I Was Growed Up Lucky

*To Inez
a Gracious Lady
God Bless You!*

Jim Cocalas

JIM COCALAS

ISBN-10: 1718969457

ISBN-13: 978-1718969452

DEDICATION

*To my wife Bobbie, who endured and blossomed,
and on November 11, 2017,
the Lord picked her for His own.*

FOREWORD

Although I met Barbara and Jim Cocalas over twenty years ago, they were a remarkable couple, and I still vividly recall my first impressions of them.

Barbara was an elegant, beautiful lady, stylishly dressed and perfectly coiffed. She spoke with an unusual accent that was a combination of 90 percent Southern belle softness and 10 percent New York twang. The moment she heard I was born in Memphis, she hugged me tightly and pronounced me her "Southern sister."

Jim was more of a mystery. He was tall, handsome with a warm, welcoming smile and gracious manners. But there was something behind his smile that I couldn't quite name. His eyes were kind, but they moved constantly as he took in every detail of his surroundings and everyone around him. He seemed to be evaluating, not in a judgmental way like some, just fully, intently present at all times. Perpetually "on duty" was the only way I could describe it. Later, I heard that he had been an NYPD cop for 30 years, a lieutenant, serving in some of the roughest areas of the city, and I thought, *Ah, that explains it.*

We entertained them and served them apple pie. They invited us to their gracious home and served us cherry pie. We bonded over ribs at the local Southern barbecue joint. I must confess that, although I loved Barbara, I had a hard time concentrating on my conversation with her about the flowers she had chosen for the church that week, while across the table Jim regaled my husband with tales of finding severed body parts in dark subway tunnels.

The years passed far too quickly, and Jim lost his precious Barbara. He was devastated. As part of his grieving process, he wrote a tribute to her and gave it to my husband, who passed it along to me. I read it. I laughed. I cried. Their love story warmed and broke my heart. But on another level, the author in me was startled to discover that my friend was a truly gifted writer! I thought of all the stories I'd heard—amusing, touching, gruesome—at the dinner table, and I was determined they would be preserved and shared. It wasn't easy, convincing Jim, but once he started writing, this book poured out of him at a rate I've never seen! His productivity put me, a seasoned author, to shame. I gave his material only the lightest edit. To do more would have ruined his charming, conversational tone. (By the way, that tribute to Barbara is the first chapter of this book.)

Once, I thought I'd enjoy being a police officer. No more. After reading this book, I see "The Job" far differently. The sadness, the ugliness, the complications of working within the departmental hierarchy, the loneliness of not being able to share the worst you've seen with anyone, not even your mate, for fear of scarring their soul, as yours has been...I don't have that kind of strength. Thank God some, like Jim Cocalas, do. What would we be without them?

Pour yourself a favorite beverage, settle down in your comfy chair, and imagine you're sitting in Jim's beautiful living room. Smell the coffee he just brewed and hear the ticking of the antique clocks that fill the house. (When the hour strikes, it's quite an event!) You can gaze into the fireplace and listen as he spins his tales for you...stories that will forever change you and give you a new appreciation of those who wear a police officer's uniform.

Sonja Massie (author, G. A. McKevett)

May 2018

BARBARA

In 1953, my buddy, Joe Lentini, and I were assigned to the USS Midway, which at that time, was in dry-dock. We were doing minor repairs, etc. We went into Portsmouth, Virginia, on liberty and ended up in an ice cream parlor. Sitting opposite us was the girl I would marry, four and one-half months from that day! I remember the date. August 4th. I think it was a Monday.

She was visiting her cousin, Ruth, after graduating high school. Ruth was divorced and had a beautiful child with her, who had an equally beautiful name, Leila. The three of them sat directly opposite us. Later, I found out that Barbara Smith, the girl I was to marry, thought that Joe was a better-looking guy than I was—until we stood up to leave, and she saw that she was a head taller than he was. (Lucky me.)

We left right after they did. Leila was getting tired, and I volunteered to carry her. Ruth had an apartment close by. I found out that Barbara lived in Kannapolis, North Carolina, and had graduated in June. She was 17 when I first saw her, and from that day on, I knew I would spend my life with her.

She stayed with Ruth for a few weeks and every day I had liberty, I went to see her and to be with her!

On one occasion, some punk got into my locker and stole my ID. You couldn't get off the ship or the base without it.

I did.

I waited until the officer on duty, who checked ID, was occupied, and I stormed down the gangway.

Okay, I thought. *Now I'm off the ship. How do I get past the marines guarding the entrances?*

A petty officer saw me, came over, and I thought, *They've got me.*

He said, "Looking to get off the base? See that green Chevy in the lot? If you can get over the fence, I'll drive you out."

I climbed over that barbed wire fence, lay down in his back seat, and we drove past the marines at the gate.

After a few blocks, he let me out.

I walked the rest of the way to Ruth's and stayed with Barbara until three in the morning! (Just talking.)

Getting back on the base was easier. The Marine didn't care if I had any ID. To him, I was just any sailor.

Now, to get on the ship.

I waited until the officer walked out of sight, then I ran like hell up the gangway, past him and into the dark hanger bay, then down to my compartment and bunk.

Was I exhausted? Yes.

Did I see Barbara that next day? You bet I did! I told you, I was going to spend the rest of my life with her.

She returned to her home in September. Her birthday was September 18. I bought a 45rpm record player for her as a present and decided to hitch a ride to Kannapolis, North Carolina, 300 miles away.

Bad move. I got stuck in one small town after another.

When I finally arrived there, after 12 hours or so, I went to the YMCA and cleaned up.

Finally, I got directions to her house. But before I could knock on the door, her friend, Gwenn, from across the street, asked if I was looking for Bobbie.

"She's at the hospital," she told me, "getting her tonsils removed."

Gulp!

I went across the street, spoke with Gwenn and waited. After a while, Bob came back with her mom. I didn't know that Bobbie's mother had a spinal problem, probably from birth. I got over that little surprise quickly and hurried across the street to meet them and give Bobbie her birthday present that I'd been lugging around for 300 miles. I loved Bob's mom from that day on.

I stayed the night, met her dad, who was a no-nonsense guy. In a little while, he took me into the backyard behind a shed and offered me a swig of white lightening out of a jar! Burned the heck out of my mouth.

Both of her parents worked at Cannon Mills. I think Bob worked there a short time. She told me years later that she would've liked to have become a nurse.

I think I stayed another full day. I remember going to a roller-skating rink and watching her skate. She was really good and I, of course, made a fool of myself.

When we left, she was backing out of the parking lot. (Imagine this: I didn't have a license, but *she* did.) She tapped a car parked behind us.

Wonderful gal that she was, she got out and put her phone number on a piece of paper so the owner could call and get her information. Bum that I was, I pretended to go back to check on the damages and removed the note.

The next day, Bobbie and her mom drove me to the bus

station. They gave me a silver bracelet with "Jimmy" inscribed on the back. I was overwhelmed.

I looked out the window to wave goodbye. Instead, I cried. (Just as I'm doing now, remembering the two of them standing there.)

When I returned to the ship, I was looking forward to seeing them again soon. But the chaplain of the ship was waiting for me.

He told me he'd received a telegram that my mom had died. I read the telegram and explained it was my girlfriend's mother.

Believe me when I tell you, that man of the cloth was annoyed that he'd had to wait for me to get back to the ship for some girlfriend's mother!

I held my temper.

I got a bus ride as soon as I could. I was too late for the funeral. I spent a day or two but had to get back to the ship.

We went to Cuba to flex our muscle.

When we got back, sometime in December, I called and told Bobbie, "Get permission from your dad to marry me, and if he says, 'Yes,' catch the next bus to Portsmouth."

He did, and she did.

She arrived with a suitcase and another matching bag. (I found out later, she'd brought her personal Bible. On the front page, she had written the day she'd received Christ as her Savior.)

I got her a room at the Portsmouth Hotel. I stayed at a boarding house and slept with the chair braced against the door; I had all the money I owned on me.

The next day was a whirlwind.

Before we could get a marriage license, we had to do a Wasserman test. (A blood test to see if you had a venereal disease.)

We took care of that, then went to a jewelry store and bought our wedding bands.

We found a church, the South Street Baptist Church in Portsmouth, and asked the pastor to marry us that day. Pastor Ellis was surprised that no one was there with us. He called the deacon of the church to be a witness, and with only the deacon and minister present, we were married.

As soon as we said our vows, we rushed off to catch the bus to Brooklyn.

On the way, we ran into some of my shipmates, who were looking for us. They'd wanted to attend the ceremony at the church.

We hurried past them to catch the bus...the bus that would take Barbara to her new life.

After 12 hours of sitting in cramped, uncomfortable seats, we pulled into the old Greyhound terminal on West 34th Street in New York City. We took the subway to Avenue M in Brooklyn and walked to my home on East 21st Street. It was about six o'clock in the morning.

My dad had already left for work, and my mom was waiting for us. I don't remember much conversation other than her asking me for the marriage license before we went to our room to sleep.

I haven't forgiven myself for putting Barbara through that ordeal—the bus ride, my mom asking for our license.

Some honeymoon!

That was December 22, 1953. We were married on the 21st. I returned to duty after Christmas.

I left my wife of less than a week with her new family: my father, Tasso, whose Greek accent was so heavy that my two sisters, Helen and Tillie, and my 15-year-old brother, Anthony, had to translate. (Just kidding.) Then there was my Uncle Chuck, who refused to allow any of his sisters to smoke, even though they were all married with several children among them.

"I don't give a damn!" he'd yell. (That's the polite version.) "Put those cigarettes out!" And that's not all he'd yell.

My sister, Tillie, told me something that may seem funny, but I found it heartbreaking....

While I was away, my mom prepared tons of food and invited her sisters and brothers (my aunts and uncles) to her home to meet Jimmy's bride from the South. After a while, Tillie went upstairs to see why Bobbie hadn't come down yet. Bobbie told her, in all honesty, she was afraid. She could hear the cursing and shouting downstairs, and she thought they were all fighting. My sister assured her they weren't. They were just being themselves.

I was supposed to be discharged in March, but since the ship was going on a cruise to the Pacific, they released me January 4, 1954! I rushed home, and we began our life in earnest.

We stayed with my parents for a few weeks more and then got a basement apartment on East 31st Street. The owners were a wonderful couple named Bello.

Shall I tell you that our daughter, Florence, was born on January 15, 1955, or that our son, James Anthony arrived on April 23, 1956? Or how I put machine shop work behind me and joined the New York City Police Department on March 16, 1957, and spent 30 tumultuous years with them? Or how our son, Philip, was born, and the Lord took him before the day was out? Or years later, when our son, Stephen, was born and the Lord took him home after ten months? Or how this affected my dear Barbara?

Maybe some other time....

LOVE CONQUERS ALL

Yes, it does, even through the Depression Era and a stint at Sing Sing Prison.

I've read biographies of people who revealed their family secrets for all the world to see, and I was always conflicted with that. Is it that important? I'll let you decide.

My father, Tassos Cocalas, was born January 2, 1902, in a Greek enclave in Smyrna, Turkey. Forced to leave because of the war between Turkey and Armenia, he emigrated to America, but not before working in France, filling the trenches left from World War I.

His dad was already in New York, waiting for the rest of his family to arrive. My grandfather had established himself as a skilled watch repairman and, eventually, bought a home in an upscale neighborhood in Brooklyn.

My dad arrived in our country and, armed with the address of where his father worked, was reunited with his dad. Thus, began my father's life in America.

My mother, Florence, was born in Brooklyn and lived in a tenement area with her mom, two brothers, and six sisters. Her dad died at an early age, and her mother struggled to keep the family safe during a very harsh time for her neighborhood and the country as a whole.

Tassos and Florence met at Coney Island on a summer day.

My dad introduced her to his parents and, eventually, he proposed marriage. She accepted but was denied a blessing from his parents, because she was not Greek Orthodox.

My father threatened to leave home.

My sister, Tillie, showed me the letters my dad wrote my mom. They were really in love.

Finally, they married in an Orthodox Church and began their life together.

Mom gave birth to my older sister, Helen, Tillie, me, and then my brother, Anthony.

Dad bought a home and opened a jewelry store with his brother, my uncle Homer.

When my brother was born, our lives crashed. It was the height of the Depression. Both my dad and my uncle were arrested for receiving stolen goods and booked in the 61 Precinct. Only my dad was sentenced. My mom always felt that my dad took a plea to protect his brother.

I heard of all this, not from my dad, nor my mom, but from my uncle, just as I was about to enter into the NYPD. (I'll tell you more about that in another chapter.)

When Dad went to prison, Mom had to move from her nice home back to her old neighborhood with four kids in tow. Later, I'll tell you how we managed to survive and how, when my dad was released on parole, he struggled to get us out of that environment.

In some ways, my parents' lives paralleled Bobbie's and mine. My grandfather didn't want my father to marry my mother. My mom didn't want us to get married. But we both had long, happy marriages. Ours lasted 63 years; theirs until my dad passed.

TWO HOMES

I was an adult when I learned that my father's family was fairly wealthy. However, their wealth had no meaning to me or my sisters. We had memories of living in a one-family home in an area of Brooklyn that even today would be called upper class, Somewhere around Ocean Parkway, close to Kings Highway.

Later, we learned that Dad and Uncle Homer had a jewelry store and watch repair in the area, I think it was at East 7th off Avenue U. We probably didn't live there too long, even though I was born in Coney Island Hospital in 1932.

I do have vivid memories of living in an apartment, where the fine furniture from the other apartment was squeezed into that one. What a contrast, where we slept three in a bed, and my infant brother was in a bassinet beside us.

The new place had no bathroom. We shared a toilet bowl with the apartment on the other side of the wall. The entrance was through a door in the kitchen. You entered and locked the other door. When finished, you'd flush and unlock their door.

Ah, yes, the kitchen. It had an ice box, which was replenished by who, other than the "Ice Man?" (Don't knock it. It was steady work.)

The cast iron stove was used for cooking and heating the apartment. Sorry. No central heating or air conditioners.

For fuel, we scrounged scraps of wood from crates in the basement that held grapes. Someone in the apartment was making wine.

No matter the season, we shared everything with our constant companions, cockroaches!

During the winter, my mom would open the oven door, put our clothes close to the stove to warm them, then wake us one at a time, to get dressed to go to school.

I often think of what my mother must have felt, having to move back into the poverty of her childhood, after her promising future with my father had crashed.

I must emphasize how destitute we were. The depression affected all in that neighborhood, but we suffered most.

As kids we had outlets. But my mom had to hang a curtain, probably a sheet, between the bedroom and the kitchen, so she could wash in the sink. She was in her late 20s, early 30s. As I'm writing this, my eyes are full of tears.

As a child, it wasn't bad at all. So what if I had holes in my shoes? My mom would take care of that, when I came home after school or playing. So what if I didn't have a toothbrush, or we slept three in a bed?

So what if I ended up in Greenpoint Hospital with pneumonia, or that a doctor drained blood from my carotid arteries after a fall, when I was an infant? (Now I know why I had scars on either side of my neck.)

Or that when we would come home at night, and my mom was about to turn on the lights, she would tell us, "Get the big ones." We knew she meant the roaches.

Are you cringing yet?

We didn't care. We had the street, the school yard, the pool at McCarran Park, sandwiches I'd never tasted before at the CYO (Catholic Youth Organization), and a container of milk.

We had open fire hydrants in the summer. Whoever had the wrench would hide it. The authorities shut the hydrant off, and, after the officials left, the kid with the wrench would turn it on again.

We played Johnny on the pony, skelly, hopscotch, kick the can, ringolevio.

I had friends with nicknames like Hooshy, Googy, Benny Lobo, and Johnny Crutch. We had a friend, Gasper, who had cerebral palsy. He was confined to a wheel chair. We doted over him.

One day, my cousin, Coony, took him to a movie on Broadway, wheelchair and all. When my cousin returned to the block, Gasper's mother let out a scream. Coony had forgotten Gasper, left him in the aisle! Coony ran back and got him. We laugh today when anyone mentions that.

Within a one block area, lived: my grandmother, her two unmarried sons, who lived with her—Uncle Chuck the oldest, Uncle Coony the youngest—my mom, and her five sisters.

It was known: "Woe be to anyone who, in any way, disrespects this family or their children!"

That edict was in effect until my dad returned. Payment for a debt.

GIVE HIM THE WORKS!—It would be too bad if a Nazi plane flew over Brooklyn while these young sailors manned an activated machine gun trainer, part of war exhibit at the Williamsburg Savings Bank. Left to right are James Cocalas, 11; Leonard Di Salvo, 13; Cono Peluso, 13, and Joseph Fontana, 11.

BROOKLYN EAGLE

Before my dad made it home, we survived whatever was thrown at us. My sisters went to an all girls' school around the corner from where we lived. As far as I can remember, they weren't affected negatively by our circumstances. They had girlfriends and boyfriends, played in the street, under the ever-watchful eyes of the neighborhood.

But we, rather I, was perplexed regarding certain thing— one of which was attending church. All my aunts and their children went to a Catholic church in the neighborhood. There were times when I attended and, without any proper instruction, I mimicked those sitting around me.

I was also exposed to the rituals of an Eastern Orthodox church in Flatbush. Unfortunately, without any guidance, religion was put on the back burner. It remained there for years, until my wife Barbara showed me THE WAY.

I enjoyed the bazaars and feasts that the churches gave, and the penny toss games they ran until, as an adult, I realized everything wasn't exactly kosher.

I was disappointed. I wanted to think that church was pristine, something special and in Technicolor. Not like the black and white stuff we saw every day in the gutter. (Know a good psychiatrist? Is he cheap?)

The place and the time we lived in produced some people who out of necessity crossed the line, committing: petty larceny, gambling, heavy drinking, robberies. And occasionally revenge killings.

On a day in 1936 at North 6th and Roebling, around the corner from where we lived, someone was shot in the street.

A famous crime photographer, Arthur "Wee Gee" Fellig took a picture of local kids gaping at the body. He had it published in *Life* magazine, naming it "First Murder." (Google it.)

On her way home from school, Tillie, saw the commotion, peeked at the dead man, and ran home to tell my mom.

Shortly after, a man known by reputation to my mom came by, spoke to her, and left.

Some time passed before I found out why he had been there.

Seems he was the man you would talk to if you had a problem. Sort of the "Quid Pro Quo" guy. He'd heard that my sister had been spotted leaving the scene right after the murder. He wanted to know what she'd seen. Fortunately, nothing.

We bought groceries from a store on the block. Whatever we bought, we would tell the owner, Sindon, "My mother says, 'Put it in the book.'"

He would take a stub of a pencil from behind his ear and write something in his book. Buy now, get paid later.

The ice man was also an important person in the neighborhood. We'd watch him cut a piece of ice, put a scrap of burlap over his shoulder, and hump the chunk of ice into one of the tenements. Once he was out of sight, we'd scurry onto his truck and grab a small piece of ice.

I must tell you about an army truck that was alongside a factory close to the Brooklyn-Queens Expressway. The soldier called us over and said, "How about a hand?"

There was no way we would refuse! We carried boxes of supplies up an outside fire escape for six flights. When we got to the top, we saw an anti-aircraft gun mounted up there.

When we were finished, he let each of sit on the gun, and he would traverse the gun as we looked through the eye piece.

Coincidently, the Williamsburg Saving Bank on Broadway near the Williamsburg Bridge had a display inside of an anti-aircraft gun (not as big as the one on the factory.)

A photographer called us in and took some pictures. They were printed in the *Brooklyn Eagle*.

I was famous!

DAD'S HOME

Once my dad came home, things improved a little. He set a table in the front room by the window and started fixing watches. He had a steady job in a machine shop and when home, he worked on the watches.

I have a ledger from when he owned the jewelry store. He was charging 25 cents, sometimes a dollar, for repairs. True it was a long time ago, but when I saw the ledger, years later, I was astonished at how little he charged.

He wasn't exactly sullen, but he wasn't talkative to some people who passed by. I'm sure he had his reasons.

We played until dark, and he would tap on the window as a signal for us to come in. He didn't tap twice.

On Saturday, my sisters and I would go to the movie on Grand Street. Mom told us to stay for the two features. It took my older sister to figure out why. Helen explained to the rest of us that our parents rarely had any privacy.

There was so much going on in our neighborhood. Things we remember and talk and laugh about it now, though it may have been sad then.

Not for me. I found the neighborhood and its characters exciting.

We had a load of peddlers come down our street. One guy had a wagon pulled by a horse, like you would see in cowboy movies. He'd pull the canvas back to show his wares.

He called himself, "Yupo." As he went down the street he would yell, "YUPO!"

My mom used to buy from him. He sold pots, pans, and most anything you would need in the kitchen.

I would sit on the curb and watch the horse relieve himself. (It definitely was a he.) I watched the animal swat flies with his tail. I watched Yupo feed him by putting a bag of oats over his head. (See what you can learn in the streets!)

There were peddlers who sold corn on the cob, cooked and then served on a piece of husk. If I got money from Mom, I would buy one and eat the corn *and* the husk!

I did the same with the watermelon. Ate the rind, too.

Years later, I related that to my friends, and it was hard to convince them it was true. They probably weren't as hungry as I was back then.

One night, we were seated at the kitchen table, a man with his face partially covered climbed in through the window.

My dad told us to stay seated and be quiet.

The man ran out our front door.

We all knew you can go from Roebling Street through a certain building into the yards and out onto North 5th Street. Apparently, this guy had been running from the cops and decided to use our house as part of his escape route.

Later, detectives came, spoke to my dad, and then left. It was all still a mystery to me, but not to my street-smart dad.

THE MOVE

Well, it was quite a time. The war brought jobs to most everyone in the neighborhood. Factories sprang up along Roebling Street, hiring local people. We weren't that far from the Brooklyn Navy Yard. You could across the Williamsburg Bridge or ride the BMT (Brooklyn Manhattan Transit) to the city, look down, and see navy ships at the piers or in the dry docks.

Years later, I found out what those ships looked like close up.

The area was a beehive of activity. Patriotism was rampant. Guys were volunteering and getting drafted.

On one occasion, they had about two hundred young guys line up along the schoolyard fence. They marched them to the subway on North 7th and Driggs Avenue. They ended up by Whitehall Street, where they were drafted into the army.

That was a sight I'll always remember.

My uncle Cooney was one of them. He served in the Pacific, came home on furlough, and got married. His unit stayed in the States until the German army made the big push on December 16, 1944. Now, we call it "The Battle of the Bulge."

His unit was called up. They arrived early in January. We didn't see him again until October 1945! If you know your history, you'll know the war in Europe was over in May 1945, and Japan signed the surrender on The USS Missouri in September 1945.

Years later, Uncle Cooney told me that his unit threatened to riot if they weren't sent home soon. (He's the uncle who would later let the cat out of the bag about my father's prison time, just as I was entering the police department.)

Getting back to the neighborhood story—there were flags everywhere. There was competition between blocks on who had the better banner that spread from one fire escape across the street to another fire escape. Huge things! The one on our street had that famous revolutionary scene called, "The Spirit of '76," with a kid playing a drum, another with a fife, and an older guy in the middle, whose head was bandaged.

They had scrap drives, victory gardens, and the big corruption system called "rationing."

Rationing books were given to families. You couldn't buy stuff that was rationed by the government, unless you had the book. When you bought something, the store owner would pull a stamp from the book. If you ran out of stamps for that particular item, too bad, unless you knew someone in the new industry that sprang up called "The Black Market."

We didn't care about gasoline rationing because—you guessed it—we didn't own a car.

Amid all this chaos, my dad decided to relocate his family.

I believe when he returned home, he already had a time table in his head for when he would move us. But first, there were obligations to be fulfilled, debts to be paid, and official notifications to be made. I think he might have needed permission from the parole board to move. We kids were oblivious to this. I'm sure my mom knew.

He reached out to my uncle Joe, my mother's sister's husband, who worked for a moving company. In keeping with the tradition of the neighborhood, my uncle helped himself to a truck when the shop was closed. Naturally. (Maybe it was the water that we were drinking?)

The truck loaded, my uncle drove from a depressed area, yet exciting and colorful, to a neighborhood with tree-lined streets and one-family owned homes. Not a factory in sight!

The truck pulled up in front of our new home, no doubt being watched by our neighbors. My dad was there, waiting. My mom and us kids were in Dad's brother's house four or five blocks south.

They started to unload. My uncle had recruited a couple of guys from the old neighborhood to give him a hand. (In those days, who wouldn't want to make a couple of bucks?)

They brought in the kitchen table and plopped it down. Out came cockroaches that scurried off the floor into any crack they could find.

"The best laid plans of mice and men."

My dad was furious. In no time my uncle Homer called an exterminator for him.

My uncle picked up Mom and us kids and brought us to our new home. We raced up and down the stairs, into the basement and up again.

Our house was the only one on the block that had a porch on the second floor overlooking the street. My mom was so happy!

In the backyard there was a fish pond. Later—much later—I took some pollywogs from a pond in Prospect Park, brought them home in a can on the train, put them in our pond, and watched nature take its course.

However, moving there wasn't all peaches and cream. Prejudice raised its ugly head. It took a while for us kids to see or feel it, but my mom and dad were well aware of it.

Let me give you my opinion on what the neighbors perceived. They saw a short, darker skinned woman—had to be an Italian—and a man who just looked foreign. They were formulating ideas and predicting the consequences of us moving to their neighborhood.

I could just imagine them saying, "And how about those kids?! They look like they're from the movies, *Dead End* or *Angels with Dirty Faces*!"

Well, my mom was 35-years-old and prettier than anyone on the block. With her head held high, she had come from a situation that they couldn't have imagined.

My dad, who traveled to the U.S.A. from war-torn Europe, was a watch repairman. He owned a jewelry close by where they lived. By necessity, he had learned to be a tool and die maker. He spoke four languages, had light skin and blue eyes.

Take *that* you prejudice bastards.

Over the years, time softened them, and they realized they had raw diamonds in their midst.

HOSPITAL STAY

Shortly, after moving into our new mansion on East 21st and while I was still getting acquainted with our new neighbors and friends, I became really sick.

My mom called a doctor. I don't know how she picked him or how she got in touch with him. He showed up and examined me in my bedroom. I had pains in my stomach.

I remember he took a stool sample, spoke to my mom, and left. He charged $2 for the home visit.

This was during our first winter there, sometime before Christmas.

Since I was still in pain and had a fever, my mom called another doctor.

After examining me, he told my mother I had to get to the hospital! My dad was at work. I think Uncle Homer took us to Coney Island Hospital, the same hospital where I'd been born. Imagine that!

Some memories are vivid. I remember being washed from head to toe. I mean it. They washed my feet and between my toes!

As they were wheeling me to the operating room, there was a black man—a fireman—sitting on a bench. He got up as I was being pushed by. He held my hand, and said, "Don't worry, I'll be giving you blood."

Was it a dream? I remember he had some gear on.

Next, I recall being in a hospital bed.

My appendix had burst. I had a yellow tube sticking out of my stomach, some sort of drain. It stank!

I asked a nurse for water. She gave me a cotton swab dipped in water, and I sucked it dry. After she left, I noticed the cup of water was within my reach. I could have drunk the whole cup, but I took a swab, dipped in the water, and sucked on it.

I remember nurses changing a huge bandage, but before putting on a fresh one, they had me move my legs up and down to force stuff out of the drain. It still stank! I don't know how many days they did this.

My mom came every day. On one occasion, she brought an orange and put it in a drawer by my bed. The night nurse was sitting at a desk with a lamp on it, reading. I was awake. She got up from the desk and was heading my way. I closed my eyes, but I peeked when she took the orange out. I guess she ate it. God bless her.

I was in the hospital at Christmas time. Santa Claus came by each bed and was giving gifts to the kids. When he got to me he gave me a doll. The nurse told him, "That's a boy." He laughed, took back the doll, and gave me an airplane. It looked like the plane Lindberg flew across the Atlantic, The Spirit of St. Louis.

I was discharged soon after. I'm guessing it was Uncle Homer who drove us home. (Have you noticed that he wasn't working? My mom had him pegged for years as a leech.)

My mom and dad gave up their bedroom so I could get sunshine while recuperating and have access to the porch. Mom got a barber from Avenue M to cut my hair at the house.

When my sisters came home from school, she warned them that the barber had cut my hair short and not to tease me or laugh at me.

They laughed.

FRIENDS, A BULLY, THE SIDESHOW, AND NATHAN'S

"You're the product of your environment," or so they say. My sisters and I found that out fast enough. The kids we started to hang out with didn't seem to be as tough as we were. But, sometimes, we were wrong.

My sisters met the Dunphy family, who lived across the street and a few houses down–Irish family, red hair and freckles.

We became close friends.

I forgot the girls' name. The boys were Jimmy and Eddy.

No doubt there were differences such as my sisters' clothes, hygiene habits, slang talk, and religion.

The Dunphys were Catholic. My sisters and I were not pushed into making any decision.

My parents were married in an Orthodox Church. My mom had been raised in the Catholic faith.

With the turmoil of moving, etc., that decision was put on a back burner.

All in all, the Dunphys became close friends for years.

As I said, my sisters got along well enough in their new surroundings. With me, it was different.

Thanks to this one kid, walking down the street was a challenge for me. Every time I walked by his house, he would come out, put me in a headlock, and give me nuggies. He was my size, but about a year older.

I mentioned this to my buddy, Dave.

"Come on, we'll straighten this out!"

Or so we thought.

The kid wrestled us *both* to ground and gave us *both* nuggies! And he was laughing, while doing it.

But he seemed to lay off me after that.

Back to my sisters' friendship with Dunphys.

The family invited the girls into their home. I wonder how their parents would have reacted if they'd known the conditions we lived in!

The friendship between our families improved slowly, as they realized we weren't going to eat their young, after all.

The guys I met were full of energy. A few of them became lifelong friends. One of them, Dave, went in the navy with me and served on the same ship. Everything we did was a big competition: who was the fastest runner, who could do more pushups, who was the strongest, (Oh yeah? Let me see *you* pick up the traffic stanchion!) and so it went.

We roamed the neighborhood, sometimes ending up at Sheepshead Bay, watching the boats tie up to the docks, checking out the fish they caught. Sometimes, they sold what they caught. There were kids diving for coins that people threw in the water. Believe or not, the water wasn't murky.

We went to Coney Island on the BMT. The fare was five cents! The first thing you'd see when you got out of the train station was Nathan's. Best hot dogs in the world!

They had a freak show on Stillwell Ave, where you stood on the sidewalk and gaped at those poor creatures. I hated that word "freak" and still do. I remember this one pair, whom they called "Zip" and "Pip." They suffered from a condition that causes a person's head to be abnormally small. In cruel, freak show lingo, they were called "pinheads." Even when I was a kid, I felt sorry for them. As an adult, with more life experience and compassion, I feel terrible, thinking of the misery those people and the others in that show must have endured.

Fortunately, that wasn't the only form of entertainment. There was the Cyclone, the Wonder Wheel, Parachute Jump, and Steeplechase Park. Heck no, we didn't go on *all* of them. If we had the money, 50 cents, we'd ride one. Usually the Cyclone. But we didn't feel sorry for ourselves about not doing more. Actually, we had more fun just horsing around together.

But, sooner or later, we had to leave. The rule was: Get home before Dad.

My home was a meeting place for my friends. My mom liked all of them. They *loved* her. Maybe because, when she would be cooking meatballs on Sunday, she would offer some to the kids. They never refused them.

DICKIE

Truthfully, unlike my sisters, I never felt any hospitality in our neighbors' homes. Quite the contrary. Especially one of them. When I called on my friend, Dickie, his mom never let me in. She'd tell me that he was doing homework.

Years later, during the Korean "conflict," he joined the army. (That just wasn't done.)

After I got out of the navy and was adjusting to civilian and married life, he showed up at my parents' house, when we all were having dinner.

My brother brought him into the kitchen. Dickie got behind me and just stood there. I asked him to sit down. He grabbed me by my throat!

My father jumped up.

I told Dad, "It's all right."

Dickie released his grip. I walked him outside and spoke to him, telling him to get some help. He may have still been in the army.

Weeks later, I got a postcard from him, saying that he had taken my advice, and he was in the Pilgrim State Psychiatric Hospital in Suffolk County on Long Island.

I went to see him. His mother was there. He was sitting on the bed.

His mom left.

I spoke to him a little longer, and then I left, too.

I never saw him again.

Around 1958, when I was in the New York City Police Department, traveling on the subway with other cops, I heard someone yelling, "Jimmy! Jimmy!"

It was my friend's mom. She sprang out of her seat and hugged me.

"How ya doing?" I asked her. "How's Dickie?"

"He's all right. He's a pharmacist out West."

When we said goodbye, she told me, "Good luck, dear friend."

FREE LUNCH

Now, back to us juvenile delinquents....

Whatever we did, we weren't malicious. However, we bent the rules a little sometimes.

On one of those occasions, the four of us went to a deli on Kings Highway and Coney Island Ave. We sat in the back booth and ordered pastrami on club with a Coke.

We ate and talked, and when I finished, I walked to the front by the register, where the owner was sitting. I stood there a bit, took a toothpick, and went outside, where I lingered in front of the store, in view of the owner.

As if by telepathy, two of my friends walked up to the register, laughing, took some toothpicks, walked innocently out the door, and stood with me.

Now here comes the acting part.

S-L-O-W-L-Y, we walked out of sight of the owner and took off.

Dave got up from the table, walked to the register, took a toothpick and plunked down two dollars for his sandwich and Coke. I don't remember how much it actually cost.

The owner told Dave it was X amount, including the price of our meals.

"What, are you kidding?" Dave asked.

The owner mentioned the fact that Dave's friends hadn't paid.

"What, they didn't pay? Hey, I only had a sandwich and a Coke," Dave said.

The owner knew it was useless to argue.

Dave paid his own bill and walked outside. He saw us up the block, laughing. He was laughing, too, but he told us, "You guys owe me two bucks."

LOST AT SEA...KINDA

When Dickie was around, he had an outboard motor, a Johnson or Evinrude. I think it was his father's, or his dad may have bought it for him. No matter. The Coast Guard told us it was meant for lake fishing.

How did the Coast Guard get involved you ask? I'll tell you....

Three of us—Dave, Dickie and I—humped the motor on a trolley car on Ocean Avenue to the last stop, Emmons Avenue, Sheepshead Bay, and turned around.

The trolley was attached to electric wires overhead, which powered it. At the end of the run, the operator would get out, pull the connection off the wire, secure it, then go to the rear and connect another set to the overhead wires. That done, off he'd go in the opposite direction. Watching him doing this was a learning experience for some future mischief that you probably don't need to hear about.

We lugged the outboard to the end of Emmons Avenue, where they rented boats.

The old timer there must have been laughing to himself when he saw how small our outboard was.

We hooked up the motor and putt-putted out of the bay toward Coney Island. I knew my family would be waiting around Bay 7.

After a while, we saw them, waving to us.

My sister swam out with sandwiches in a plastic bag. (God bless my mom.) That was no easy feat for my sister. She hung onto the side of the boat until the lifeguards whistled us away.

We reversed the boat and noticed that the tide was moving us out toward the jetty, which protected the bay from the Atlantic. You guessed it. The outboard wasn't powerful enough.

Not to worry. The jetty was a way off.

But in minutes we knew we were in trouble. (A lousy feeling.)

No matter how we tried to go this way, the tide took us that way.

We drifted past where the jetty ended and were swept into the Atlantic.

We threw out the anchor but were still being pulled out.

After what seemed like an eternity, but was in reality about ten minutes, the Coast Guard showed up and towed us back into the bay.

Before leaving, they told us that outboards were for lakes, and that guy who rented us that water-logged boat should have known better.

Lesson learned.

IN THE HANDS OF THE LAW

One summer day, we went to the beach. My older sister, Helen, who was pregnant with her first child was there with her husband, Ray. Davie and I and a couple of other guys went to get some sodas being sold on the boardwalk.

We were stopped by a man who flashed a badge and said, "You aren't allowed on the boardwalk with just a bathing suit on." He also mentioned it would only be a five dollar fine.

Somebody said they wanted to see the badge again. We didn't believe he was a "police officer" and told him to take a walk.

He followed us down onto the beach.

Some words were exchanged.

He turned as if to walk away, when suddenly, he whipped around and pointed a gun at us. (Yep, he was legit!)

He marched all five of us in our bathing suits to the 60 Precinct.

My sister was quite upset and let the officer have a good piece of her mind. (She'd been left stranded with our clothes.) Her words would have made a sailor blush.

They kept us locked up and told us we were going to night court. My father showed up at the precinct with our clothes.

We rode to court in a paddy wagon. Court was in Manhattan at 100 Centre Street.

Believe it or not, the judge sided with us. The officer was steaming.

Years later, when I applied for the NYPD, I had to get an affidavit from the police officer, explaining what had happened and that I wasn't a threat to society.

By then, he was a sergeant.

He did the right thing.

RUTH BADER GINSBURG, ME, AND SWIMMING NAKED

I went to James Madison High School. That's in Brooklyn on Bedford Avenue. Ruth Bader Ginsburg, the Supreme Court Justice, was in my graduating class. We must have passed each other in the hallways. I honestly don't remember her. I'm pretty sure she doesn't remember me. That was in June of 1950. She went on to bigger things, while I went on to, well, things.

My buddies were Walter Nizick, Danny Jacobson, Dickie Weiss, Herbie Grolnick, and Davie Auerbach.

Later, Davie and I went into the navy and served on the USS Midway together.

As a teenager, Walter always celebrated Christmas with my family. My mother made sure he had a gift to unwrap. When the Korean "conflict" began, he was drafted into the marines. He was wounded twice and was awarded the bronze or silver star. I don't know which. He never talked about it.

Many years later, Walter reached out to me. He was living

alone on Ocean Avenue, had never gotten married. Sometime after that, I went to his apartment to invite him to a poker game. I knocked on his door and was told he didn't live there anymore. Later I found out from my dentist, "Doc" Silverberg, that Walter had diabetes and died a few weeks after his visit to me. That bothered me for a long time.

But all those sad times were in the future and the summer of 1950, our biggest concern was how to entertain ourselves.

Come summer, most of our friends would go to camp. I wondered, *What the heck is that all about?*

It seemed to me that, rather than have their little darlings hang out in the "mean streets" of Flatbush during the summer, their parents sent them to camps run by various religious groups.

Us heathens–Dave, Danny, and I–had to make do while they were gone.

What to do? What to do?

We came up with a solution to our woe, swimming in the high school pool.

Oops. We found out it was closed for the summer.

But not for us.

One particular summer night, we "discovered" an unlocked window facing the playing field, a bit high.

I got a boost up, climbed in, and opened a door for Dave and Danny.

The pool itself was locked, so we explored.

We played around in the gym on the fifth floor. We found the back door to the pool—two doors really, chained loosely together.

We discovered, if we pulled hard enough, the two would come apart at the top, creating an opening. I was the only one who could squeeze through. They had to climb five flights, go across the gym, and back down again to get to the front entrance, where I was waiting to let them in.

We hadn't planned it that carefully. We had no bathing suits or towels. We swam, bare ass, all week. (No, Ruth wasn't there. So much for my sexy, tell-all book.)

Until one night, the custodian caught us and called the cops. We scooped up our clothes, ran out of the building, and raced across the baseball field. Danny, who was on the school's football team, slipped in some mud at second base.

We hid under the stands as a patrol car played its spotlight on the field. We didn't go back.

What made us do stuff like that?
Like I said, I think it was the water.

JOBS

Boring! With most of my friends frolicking at camp and school closed for the summer, it was going to be a dull couple of months. Dave's father came up with a solution for me. I suspected he thought I was a bad influence on Dave. Truth was, they were trying to influence me with their politics.

I know his mom was listening to the radio every time I called for Dave, and she tried to get me involved in a discussion on politics and world events.

One day, I signed something she gave me. It may have been a petition of some sort. I guess today you might call Dave's parents "left wing radicals."

What the heck did I know?

I should have known because in a few months, after talking to my neighbors, some guys in suits came and questioned me. They must have figured out that I didn't know a communist from a pastrami sandwich.

Back to my jobs....
When I was seventeen, I started delivering radio grams. I reported to the office in the Chrysler Building on East 42nd Street. No easy task to get there from Brooklyn. You had to take the BMT to the 34th Street station and either walk to 42nd Street or take the subway. Then take the shuttle to Grand Central Station (all this for a nickel) and walk a few blocks east to the building. I had to report to the lower lobby. You wouldn't call it "the basement." Not in that beautiful building.

I reported to someone behind a counter, who asked for my working papers. To get them, you went to 110 Livingston Street in Brooklyn, took a physical, and they'd let you know your restrictions: where you could work, hours, etc.

I would sit on a bench with older guys, maybe retirees, until they called me.

My turn.

"Make sure you get a receipt!" they'd say.

I would find the address, deliver the radio gram, get a receipt. No tip.

I'd return to the office, give the guy his receipt, and sit down until I was called again.

Not exactly brain surgery, but what the heck. I was getting paid 79 cents an hour. (Was it really that low? Yeah, look it up.)

Anyway, one day, while delivering a radiogram, I felt an urgent need to urinate. If you've ever had that feeling, you know what I'm talking about. I was close to a construction site by the East River and relieved myself behind this big stone.

Okay, I can't sugar coat it.

I peed on the cornerstone for the future United Nations Building!

Enough said.

One last comment: While working there, I never received a tip, until I was delivering to a building on 42ⁿᵈ Street, close to the East River. I entered the lobby, got on the elevator, and went to the apartment. I knocked. A guy opened the door. I remember he had a foreign accent, possibly German.

He signed the receipt and gave me a dime tip!

As I was walking back to the elevator, I dropped it. It rolled into the space in the floor in front of the elevator.

It's probably still there.

If you find it it's mine.

Beside that job and delivering stuff for the Whelan's Drug Store on Ocean Avenue and Avenue M, on certain weekends, I would jump in the back of Albert's fruit and vegetable truck. He dealt with the wealthier homes around Bedford Avenue. I would take orders.

Albert would tell me, "Don't forget, use the side door."

"Okay."

The ladies would tell me, "Give me a dozen oranges, six Macintosh apples, a pound of grapes, and they better be ripe, or I don't want them!"

"Yes, ma'am."

I'd go back to the truck and start filling the order. Albert would add up the price and give me enough change in case they gave me a twenty.

On some of those deliveries I would get a quarter tip!

After he made the rounds, he would pull up to my home on East 21ˢᵗ and drop me off. I always rode in the back of the truck. Before I jumped off I'd sneak a small bag filled with fruit.

He'd yell, "See you tomorrow."

"Okay, Albert."

I think he knew.

If you're not bored yet, I'll tell you one more about a job Dave and I did for a couple of weekends.

This guy on my block knew me from watching us play touch football and me going and coming up the block. I knew he was in the army. He was about 35 or so and when he saw me, he'd always say, "How're doing?"

This day he was sitting on his stoop, and he called us over. "How would you like to make a couple of bucks each?"

Before we could answer, he continued, "And after we're finished we could shoot some shotgun rounds."

"Sure!" Who the heck wouldn't?

He explained he belonged to a skeet shooting club and needed a couple of guys to load the skeet traps.

I'd seen skeet shooting in Pennsylvania before.

Dave had a blank look on his face. I explained it to him later.

"All right," the guy said, "I'll see you tomorrow at about ten."

We showed up, and he drove us up Kings Highway quite a way and then headed east toward the Belt Parkway, about where Starrett City was to be built.

He pulled over and parked. There were about ten or so guys hanging out. Men in their 40s and older, smoking, gathered around this table where the mechanism that released the clay pigeons was set up.

There were a couple of buildings, shacks really, one about ten-feet-tall and a smaller one. He took us into the shorter of the two and showed us how it worked. You put a clay pigeon on an arm which would be pulled back and then released electronically by the guy at the table, when the shooter yelled, "Pull!"

Whoosh, out it went through an opening in the shack.
BANG!

I took the taller shack. Inside it had boxes of clay pigeons. It was hot and had a wasp nest in a corner.

Okay, I told myself. *Here we go! Load the arm. Hear the*

guy yell, "Pull!"
BANG!
Load again. Guy yells, "Pull!"
BANG!
Once in a while, there was a defected one that shattered.
Load again. "Pull!"
BANG!
This time the pellets hit the building I was in. The shack was covered with tin to prevent any penetration, but it scared the bejasses out of me!

In less than an hour, we stopped. They gave us some water. And as he'd promised, he handed me a .410-gauge shotgun and had a guy release some clay pigeons.

I'd fired shotguns before, so I hit a couple of them.

Dave? No.

On the way back in the car the guy (You should know by now that I don't remember his name.) asked, "How was it? Wanna do it again next weekend?"

"Sure!"

Next weekend we came prepared. We brought a thermos of water, ear plugs and some lunch. I figured out how to trigger the arm so it would whoosh out a fraction of a second sooner, just as the guy was going to mouth, "Pull!"

Miss!

I heard some loud talking by the table.

I couldn't do again for a while.

I watched the shooter through a crack, waited, and then did it one more time. I released the pigeon just as he was yelling, "Pull!"

BANG!

A miss! More yelling!

At the end of the day the guy paid us off. As he was driving us home he told me, "I know you did it. I don't like that guy you did it to anyway."

Dave didn't know what he was talking about.
When we got out, we asked, "Next week?"
"No."
It must have been the water.

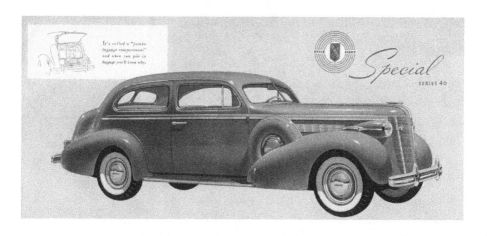

JOY RIDE

My first car was a 1937 Buick, which I bought for $10 from a guy who hung around a pharmacy where I worked as a delivery boy—the Whalen Drugstore on Avenue M and Ocean Avenue. This was in 1948, when I was 16 years old.

The car was black; they were all black in those days. It had a stick shift and about a quarter tank of gas. Gasoline was 25 cents a gallon!

He had it parked on Ocean Avenue. I gave him the $10, put some cardboard plates on it, and went to pick up two of my friends, Dave and Danny. (I had learned to drive my uncle's truck in Pennsylvania.)

We picked up a young girl we all knew (not in the biblical sense.) I don't remember her name. She was a sweet, fun-to-be-around girl.

We had fun, driving around in Flatbush, staying off the large avenues.

On one occasion I was driving, and Dave and Danny were in the back seat with the girl. The car seemed sluggish and we thought maybe it needed some gas. So, we pulled into a station at Avenue U and Flatbush Avenue.

As we drove up to the pumps, smoke started billowing out from under the car.

There was a cop assigned to that intersection. He was approaching us fast, yelling, "Move that car away from the pumps!"

Danny leaned across the seats and shouted at me "You've got the emergency brake on!"

(That explained the sluggishness and the clouds of smoke.)

I released the brake.

Danny yelled "Get out of here!"

I put the car in gear and pulled out onto Flatbush. I could hear the cop shouting. I crouched low behind the wheel, sure he was going to start shooting any minute! I could just feel a bullet hitting me between my shoulders!

What would my mother say?

I made a left onto a side street in a residential area of one-family homes.

I pulled over, shaking like a leaf. "Danny," I said, "you drive."

We switched seats.

He turned down a street, where a few cars were double parked. It turned out there was a party in one of the houses.

He was going slow through the narrow space, but I noticed he was getting a little close to the cars on my side.

"Danny, you're too close," I said. "*Danny, you're too close!*"

I heard that sickening sound of metal against metal, and I wasn't the only one. People poured out of one of the houses.

I grabbed the girl, and we ran around the corner. I told her to wait there. Then I rushed back into the war zone.

They had Danny by the throat, and Dave pinned against the car. They seemed to know what they were doing. (Um...let's just say this was an Irish neighborhood.)

An older man came out, and he calmed things down. "Who owns this car?" he wanted to know.

"I do," I said.

"Have you got insurance?"

"No."

He turned to some of the fellas who had been about to teach us a lesson, "Help these guys separate the cars."

We got them apart.

Then the man told us, "Get outta here."

We did.

Oops. Sorry.

THE NAVY
NEEDS YOU!
DON'T **READ**
AMERICAN HISTORY~
MAKE IT!

U·S·NAVY RECRUITING STATION
34 EAST 23rd ST., NEW YORK

WE'LL TAKE YOU!

My buddy, Dave, and I were just hanging out, discussing what we were going to do about work or going into the service or whatever.

In our senior year, "Log Book," where every graduate writes down their future plans, Davie said he was going into the French Foreign Legion. Some character.

Then here came Brucie Parker in a U.S. Air Force uniform.

"Don't tell me you signed up for four years!" we said.

"No. I joined the reserves and activated myself for active duty for just two years."

(You see, no one wanted to get drafted. They could put you in the marines! If you signed up for the navy or the Air Corp, that meant four years!)

"Where did you sign up?" we asked.

"Floyd Bennett Field," he told us.

Dave and I hopped on a bus on Flatbush Avenue, going to Floyd Bennett, and proceeded to the recruiting office.

We spoke to an Air Corp recruiter, and he informed us that the quota for the reserves was full.

Before we could react, a recruiter for the U.S. Navy, sitting at a desk on the other side of the room, said, "We'll take you."

And they did.

When I told my mother I'd joined the navy, she wanted to kill me.

My father understood. On my 21st birthday, I received a letter from him. I was on the USS Midway at the time. (I cherished that letter. I still have it.) But that was later.

Dave and I took "boot camp" training right there at Floyd Bennett! After six weeks or so, they sent us home to await further orders.

It was embarrassing!

Walter was drafted into the marines. Dickie Weiss joined the army. And Dave and I were back on Kings Highway, eating pastrami on club.

After a few months, they sent us to Willow Grove Naval Air Station, just outside of Philadelphia.

Another country club.

Then we volunteered for sea duty.

After another couple of months, we got orders to report to Norfolk Virginia Receiving Station and await the arrival of the USS Midway.

Now we're getting somewhere!

Or so I thought.

MY FIRST (LEGITIMATE) CAR

When I decided it was time for my first car, (one that I could tell my mom about) I reached out to my brother-in-law mechanic, Ray, who worked in a dealership in Brooklyn.

Let me tell you about him....

In the later part of the war, he and my sister were seeing each other. You know, boyfriend/girlfriend. He was drafted and his outfit was in Luxembourg.

As they approached a small, bombed-out town, they did what, according to him, all soldiers did. They started looking for "souvenirs."

He came across a shop that, at one time, may have been a jewelry store.

He and others were scavenging, and he picked up some watches and stuffed them in his pants. He knew about watches from my father.

Later, Ray's unit was crossing a field and got caught in a barrage that blanketed the field.

He was hit with a piece of shrapnel in lower part of his stomach. He told me, as he was lying in the snow, he thought he would bleed out before the medics got to him.

He passed out and woke in a field hospital, where they stripped him, pants and all. (Sorry, brother-in-law-to-be.)

He survived and made it home.

The two love birds eloped.

Skip ahead a few years: They produced two kids, Ray Jr. and Laura.

His true character came out over the years. He was a gambler and, worse, a womanizer, which caused Helen to divorce him.

Good riddance!

Oh, yeah. He helped me buy my first legitimate car, a 1951 Chevy.

UNCLE HOMERS
HUNTING LODGE

BIG GAME GARANTED
POKER TOO

WORKING STIFF

Well, I got the car, brought it home, showed it to Bobbie and my Dad. I had to get a driver's license. No problem. While my Dad was checking the car out, I asked him if he would like to drive it around the block.

"No."

He directed the conversation to something about the car.

I realized, for the first time in my short life, that my Dad didn't have a license! He was only fifty-two.

Now, I know there was more to it than just, "No."

Years later, it was all made clear.

At my first try, I got a job in a small shop close to home. We made frames for pocket books.

I really didn't want to reveal this, but on an election day I thought you were supposed to get two hours to vote. So, I left two hours early. Dope.

Next morning, the owner "let me go." Polite for "being fired." When I tried to explain, I realized how lame I sounded. (You knew I wasn't really going to vote, didn't you?)

I don't remember telling Bobbie.

I sure didn't tell my Dad.

I got another job in a shop on Third Avenue in Brooklyn. I worked there for a while. It was okay, except they were using our small locker to store parts.

I was one of the few guys who would use the room to change from clean clothes to work clothes.

I mentioned it to my foreman. He looked me in the eyes and said, "Don't make a big deal out of it."

Oh-oh. A cryptic warning.

On our morning breaks, we'd all rush out to get a small coffee, grab a quick smoke, and then head back to the shop.

The next morning, somebody was sitting in a car, watching us.

As I approached the side door to the shop, he got out. A big guy!

"Are you Cocalas?"

"No."

I went into the shop.

The foreman didn't make eye contact or conversation the whole rest of the day. The guy wasn't there when I left.

Next morning, there he was, sitting in the car. Same spot.

At the coffee shop I called my navy buddy, Dave.

"Meet me at the shop and bring a bat," I told him.

He asked me, "What gives?"

I gave him the rundown on what I thought was going to happen.

He showed up and parked a little behind the guy. I walked out of the shop with a large wrench, and the big guy got out of the car.

Dave climbed out of his vehicle with the bat in his hand.

The big guy looked at Dave, looked at me, gave me a sort of smirk, got back in his car and drove away.

Was I neurotic or did I have good survival Instincts?

I packed my tools and left.

Before I could find another job, the Devil showed up—my cousin, Homer. "Just got in," he said. "Got a great job putting tile up in new houses out in Islip."

I should have run.

About four or five years older than I was, Homer had been my earthly mentor all my teen years.

He lived in Brooklyn with his parents, my aunt and uncle, and his three sisters, until they skipped town, leaving the owner of the house they rented holding the bag.

They moved to a small town in Pennsylvania, and my uncle used all his wiles to captivate the town. He ran for sheriff, opened a gas station, raised chickens, and sold soda and ice cream off their porch.

He advertised in Brooklyn that he was running a hunting lodge and would guarantee big game on his property.

Anyone who showed up was fed by my aunt and given a cot in a small space they'd converted into a dormitory. Before these "hunters" went to bed my uncle would entice them into a little poker game.

Well, like father, like son.

Homer conned me: "Work with me, putting up tiles, and you'll make twice as much as I'm making now."

Bovine Scatology. (General Schwarzkopf said that to someone during the Kuwait War.) It sure was.

I lasted a while.

Two good things came out of it. First, I met the owner and, one day, while we were working together, he related a story about the plight of his family during the depression—no money and bad overcrowding in the tenement where they lived.

He had been in his late teens and decided to leave home, giving his father a break. He made it to a truck terminal in the city, hitched a ride, and he was on his way across the country.

He had no definite destination, just moving from place to place, wherever he could find a meal and wash up. He said he was always clean shaven, kept his hair cut, and sometimes would wash in diner rest rooms, after having a cup of coffee.

He made it to the West Coast and, after a while, he worked on a ship that went through the Panama Canal back to the New York Harbor, and then he returned to his home. After a short stay, he left and did the trip again.

Back then...when men were men.

His name was Augie Piazza.

The second good thing was, I left that job. For a good reason.

One of my teenage friends, Jerry T, became a police officer, a well-respected job in the 1950s.

When I met him, I hit him with a barrage of questions.

"How did you do it?

"I took the test."

"What test?"

"The civil service test."

"How did you know there was a test?"

"I read it in *The Chief.*"

"What's *The Chief?*"

"It publishes all the civil services jobs—Fire Department, Sanitation, Transit, and the dates of upcoming tests."

"That's for me!"

The test for NYPD was coming up soon. I was about 24, had two kids, shoveled snow the previous winter for money, and took a job as a roofer's helper, but I was intent on passing the test.

There was a school called Delahantys, that was run by former officers. They helped you prepare for the test. It was on East 31st Street in Manhattan. You would take a class and then go to the roof, where they had a small track.

I was determined to pass all three phases: the written test, the medical and the physical. (As a side note, I was worried about the eye test.)

On the day I was to take the medical, they put me in a room to fill out a questionnaire. On the wall was an eye chart. The 20/20 line read D E S P O T I C. I aced it. (Next time you're in a doctor's office, check out the 20/20 line. It still spells out "despotic.")

I passed all three phases and received a mark, which was the basis of the list number. The higher the number, the faster you'd get called.

I was waiting anxiously for that call.

I still needed to make money to pay my $50 a month rent to Mr. Bello.

While waiting, I answered an ad for a roofing company called Tilo. You had to shape up each morning and just take whatever you could handle.

The first day, I was sitting on a bench in an office when they said, "I got a roofer's assistant job on a three-story Tudor."

Nobody moved. So, I raised my hand. He gave me the address.

I had all the tools I needed in my car, a hammer and a roofing knife. The address was around East Second and Ditmas Avenue. I pulled up and spotted the ladder stretching up three stories.

I climbed it and saw a little dwarf of a man, hammering away.

He said, "Come on up." He was on scaffolding, which he'd hammered into the roof.

I climbed up the ladder, onto the scaffolding and started working, peeking over the edge of the roof down to the concrete driveway.

After a short time, the scaffold, which he'd nailed on, came loose and toppled to the ground.

He slid down to the gutter and hung on.

He laughed at me, lying as flat as I could, and said, "Slide to the ladder."

I did and was on my way down.

He got onto the ladder and was about four or five rungs above me, when the knife he had been using fell out of his belt, hitting me on the forehead.

I got a nice cut.

He took me to a luncheonette. I put some napkins on the still-bleeding wound. He ordered some barley soup for us. It was the first barley soup I'd ever eaten. It was delicious. To this day, I love barley soup.

So, napkins on my bloody head, I ate my barley soup and went home.

He'd put me in for a full day.

You think that's all that happened to me that day?

Bruce Parker's cousin, who took the same test I did, but scored lower on the list, came to my basement apartment.

"We're going to be sworn in next week!" he told me, ecstatic.

"Can't be!" I said. "I haven't heard anything yet. I had a higher mark and was higher on the list!"

He left mumbling, "I'm sorry."

Think I slept well that night?

In the morning, I went to Manhattan and up to the Department of Personnel's office. I think it was in City Hall.

I entered and literally confronted them. There were three old men sitting at a long desk, covered with papers.

I explained the disparity in my friend's mark and mine and the fact that he'd been called up before me.

They hit me below the belt by bringing up the fact that I was arrested in Coney Island with others, back when I was a teenager.

I pleaded my case: "I was 16. I'm 25 now, married with two children. I have an honorable discharge from the navy."

They relented. Sort of.

"Just get a disposition from the arresting officer," they said, "and have him explain the results of the case."

I was devastated, but more determined than ever.

I found out he was a sergeant in the 63 Precinct. (I think.) I made an appointment to meet him.

He remembered the incident. I explained I was a kid, that I'd served in the navy, and was married with two kids.

He wrote out a favorable report.

I was back on the list but had to wait six months for the next class.

In the meantime, I still had to pay Mr. Bello's his $50 every month for rent.

BIRTHDAY WISH

⚓ ⚓ ⚓

Here is what my dad sent me on my 21st birthday, while I was in the navy.

"And this is all I'd have you be, true in all you say or do,
Then no shame can come to you.
This I have you bear in mind, it is better to be kind, generous of heart,
Than to hurt, to be smart.
Skill and strength I'd have you own, but don't trust to them alone.
It is better to be fair than the costlier medal wear.
Play your game to win, but choose never self-respect to lose.
Be a man and be a friend, down into your journey's end."

WELCOME TO THE NAVY

⚓ ⚓ ⚓

After Dave and I joined the navy, they had a ceremony at Floyd Bennett Airfield in Brooklyn. We were assigned a barracks shared with mostly guys from Brooklyn and a few from out of town.

I remember one of them was a big guy from Edna, Texas. We got outfitted with uniforms and other gear and were told, "We'll have 'boot camp' here at the airfield."

Most guys were happy about that. Not me. Boot camp is similar to basic training in the army. It was supposed to toughen you up, teach you military methods of doing things, discipline us, behavior, and duties aboard ships etc.

It was a piece of cake. It was too easy. (Sounds crazy, right?) I guess I wanted more of a challenge.

We had classes on procedures, dress codes. We marched around the parade grounds with wooden replicas of real rifles.

Smart move on their part. Some of these guys I wouldn't trust with the real thing. I guarantee you, one of those guys would have tried to sell theirs. Hey, don't forget, this was Brooklyn.

We had a gym and were given exercises by a chief petty officer named Steve Belloise. Quiet guy, soft spoken, never really give us a hard time. (He could have. We had a lot of jokers in our barracks.)

One day, I was in the gym sparring, with another sailor, a friend of mine. The chief was watching and asked if I wanted to put on the gloves with him.

"Sure," I said.

Wrong answer.

I figured he was in his 40s, and we would just work up a sweat.

That was my second mistake. The first was thinking he was a doddering old man in his 40s.

He was 33, a veteran of WWII and a former professional boxer, who had fought Ray Robinson, a welter weight and middle weight champ in the 1940s! (Do you think I would have stepped in the ring if I'd known that beforehand?)

When they rang the bell, I saw a transformation like you see in the movies. He came at me in a crouch. I poked a jab at him, and he hit me with a left hook, knocking me down. I stayed down, not really hurt, but I knew that getting up would give me the same.

Thus, ending my boxing career.

WILLOW GROVE

⚓ ⚓ ⚓

We completed our "boot camp" and got orders to report to the Willow Grove Air Station. It was close to Philadelphia, PA and was just as it sounded–quaint.

It was close to a small place called "Germantown." The community was like a Norman Rockwell painting. The store windows were painted with Thanksgiving themes: stalks of corn, pumpkins, figures in Pilgrims' clothes. There were ice cream parlors, gift shops...you get the idea.

There was a combination dance hall, hang out, barn-type building just outside of the town, where they served non-alcohol drinks, hot dogs, hamburgers. Strictly supervised.

I often thought they should try that in NYC. On the other hand, it would never work. What was I thinking?

On the base, we actually worked on planes. Mostly, they were WW2 types, such as the Corsair, which was used in the

Pacific. We were taught how to adjust the carburetors, while
the engines were running, sitting in the cockpit, revving up
that powerful engine, learning to double check any bolts
you'd adjusted, and making sure the cowling was secured
with the dzus buttons. (Got you on that one. It's a real word,
pronounced "zoos.")

We had planes on the tarmac, which had to be guarded at
night. There were three shifts: 4 p.m. to midnight, midnight
to 4 a.m., and 4 a.m. to 8 a.m.

My first time on watch, I had the midnight to 4 a.m. shift.

They drove you out in a jeep with an officer, who would
supervise the changing of the guards.

The guards were issued .45 automatics with live ammo.
The guy I was relieving turned it over to the officer, who
removed the clip, pulled back the slide, and checked to see
if it was empty. Then he slammed back the clip and handed
it over to me, along with the duty belt and holster.

Before they left, the driver warned me. "When you hear
the chain drop at the entrance to the air field, it means the
officer is making his rounds."

They left, and I started my watch.

I inspected the doors of a small office building. I checked
the perimeter of a few planes on the tarmac making sure they
were secured.

It was getting real cold.

I went back to that office and used my pen knife to release
the lock on the door. (Don't look so shocked. It's easy.) Once
inside I flipped on the overhead heater, flopped in a chair,
putting my feet on the desk.

After a while, the Roy Rogers came out of me, and I took
out the .45.

Like a dope, I pulled back the slide slightly, causing a
round to leave the clip. It was almost in the barrel.

The smart thing would have been to remove the clip, pull

back the slide completely, and the round would have flopped out. Genius that I was, I figured I could push it back in the clip with my thumb.

Two things happened.

I heard the chain drop.

And my thumb was stuck!

TOTAL PANIC!

I shut off the heater, still trying to free my thumb.

The jeep stopped in front, and I realized the officer was probably looking for me.

He jiggled the door handle. I slammed flat behind a cabinet. (Yep, thumb still stuck.)

He poked his head in for a fast look, then left, got back in the jeep, and rode on.

I freed my thumb, went outside, and resumed my watch.

The jeep came back. The officer called me over.

He didn't say a word. Just felt my pea coat (still warm) and left.

MUTINY ON THE MIDWAY

⚓ ⚓ ⚓

When I first saw the ship, it was in the harbor. They took us out in a whaleboat and as we got closer, it sort of scared me! It was huge! On the smokestack was painted the numbers "41."

We pulled alongside the gangway, went up the ladder, saluted the flag, and asked the project officer for "permission to come aboard, sir."

"Granted," he said. "Find yourself a bunk and report to So-and-So in the morning."

Easier said than done.

We were in what is called the "hangar bay." That's the area where they store the planes. It was huge!

We found a compartment with some empty "racks" and settled in for the night.

In the morning we reported to an office and were interviewed by an officer. I told him, "I went to airplane mechanic school."

He said, "fine."

I pushed planes. I pushed them on the elevators. I push them off the elevators. I push them onto the flight deck. I push them into the hangar bay. And when we had no planes on board, we chipped paint. Never once did I take a tool to a plane's engine is all the time I was on board.

By stroke of luck, I managed to transfer to the machine shop. I met a great bunch of guys there. Leo Seeley, Jim Harshberger, and others, whose names are rattling around in my head. Hey, it was over 50 years ago! Anyway, my time on board was an experience I wouldn't trade for anything. I traveled to France, Italy, Greece, Spain, Algiers, Scotland, Guantánamo Bay, Gibraltar, Haiti, and Nova Scotia.

We sailed past the Arctic Circle, all through the Mediterranean. I guess I did everything a sailor is supposed to do except to get a tattoo. I was afraid of needles.

Before I go any further, I didn't forget that there was a real war going on in Korea. So, don't think I'm complaining. We had good chow, clean racks, hot showers. And best of all, no one was trying to kill me. (Except this one petty officer.)

I was on a work detail, and we got into an altercation. As I was climbing out of the storage hole, he shoved me down with his foot. I struck him. Bad move!

In about 15 minutes, the master at arms came down, looking for me. I was handcuffed. I was brought before the commanding officer. I was in awe of him! I heard him say, "You striking that petty officer was like you striking me." I tried to speak, but all I heard was, "You are sentenced to three days bread and water in solitary confinement." I immediately thought of the movie, *Mutiny on the Bounty* and almost started to giggle.

Well, I wasn't giggling when they closed that cell door. A Marine was seated right in front of the cell. He gave me a form to read regarding my behavior while in custody. No talking, singing, smoking. (Singing?)

Reveille was at 5 a.m. lights out was 10 p.m. There was a Bible and a stool in the cell. So, what was the first thing I did? I asked the Marine for a cigarette. Bad move! He opened the cell door, pulled me out, slammed me against the bulkhead. (That's "wall" to you landlubbers.) He pulled out his sidearm and put it against my head! "Didn't you read that form?" He yelled in my ear. "NO TALKING!" I didn't talk for the next three days.

Well, so much for the host of this establishment, I thought. The accommodations were sparse. However, the room service was good. I had another prisoner arrive at breakfast and ask me, "What'll you have?"

I said, "What's on the menu?"

"Bread and water," he said.

"I'll take one of each."

Sure enough, he returned with one slice of white bread and a cup of water. And so it went for the remainder of my stay.

Rest assured, I wouldn't be coming back.

On Sunday, my last day, a guy brought me two cups with a slice of bread on each. When I looked in the cups, one of them had orange juice and the other had black olives! God bless him!

When my time was up, and they let me out of the brig, the first guy I saw was my buddy, Joe Lentini. He was waiting for me to get out, and he had some chicken for me from the last meal. Great guy!

Years later, while patrolling in Times Square, I saw the man who had given me the orange juice and olives walking down the sidewalk. I stepped in front of him without saying a word. He stared at me and finally recognized me. We hugged each other. It seemed strange to people watching us, a white cop and a black man hugging and laughing on W. 42nd Street in the late 50s. I never saw him again, but I won't forget him nor his name, Reginald Benedict Lewis.

BATTLE OF NORFOLK

⚓ ⚓ ⚓

While the ship was still in dry dock, way before I met Bobbie, I went on liberty with one of my shipmates by the name of Kearns. We took the ferry to Norfolk. It was a more active town than Portsmouth.

We didn't drink, so we hung around and ended up in a coffee shop, where we had some burgers.

It was nice being off the ship, although I remember we got chastised by a policeman for crossing the street before the light changed. Oops! Didn't he realize, we were America's guardians against those North Korean hordes?

We returned by ferry. I was leaning against the bulkhead, when three drunken sailors approached me. After a bit, they started getting physical. Lucky for me, they had Shore Patrol assigned on the ferry.

My buddy came running up and asked what happened. I wasn't hurt, but I started to pull his leg. "Where the heck were you? Those guys would have killed me!"

He got steamed and was going after them. The Shore Patrol stopped him.

Once we docked, the drunken trio left, walking up the main street. We followed and confronted them.

I was getting caught up in the moment when—

Whack!

Somebody from behind hit Kearns and knocked him to the ground. The guy's momentum caused him to stumble over Kearns, and he landed in the street with me all over him.

Someone grabbed my jersey and spun me around. It was one of Portsmouth's finest. I shrugged him off and kept on swinging.

When I awoke, I was in the back of a paddy wagon. (They had them down South, too.)

They took Kearns to a hospital.

When my head cleared, I recognized the sailor they were putting in the van with me. One of the three.

I hit him, which got me a seat in the front with handcuffs.

At the station, it was a case of, "He said, I said," and they cut me loose.

I went to the hospital—don't know how—and found Kearns in a hospital bed with a swollen jaw and a lump on his head.

I said to him, "We've got to get back to the ship! Come on!"

With a little help we made it back.

What's that saying? "When men were men," or something like that?

PLANE PUSHER

⚓ ⚓ ⚓

I believe I mentioned before that I told the lieutenant on the USS Midway about my qualifications as an air plane mechanic, and how he conned me into thinking I was going to be handling planes.

The truth was...the squadron brings aboard everything they need, except plane pushers.

What are plane pushers, you ask? I'll tell you.

After a squadron lands on board, we push the planes quickly onto an elevator, which takes them below to the hanger bay. Then we pack them close to other planes, actually inches apart.

When they were all secure, we, the plane pushers, returned to our other duty, which was chipping paint with hand chisels, scrappers, and sanders. When we were down to the bare metal, we'd paint over what we had just finished. (Can you guess the color?)

When at sea, they might have to launch planes. Easy for us. Just reverse the order. Push planes onto the elevator. Then off the elevator onto the deck, where they were attached to a catapult.

Now, here was where it got tricky and dangerous. Sometimes, when they'd overshoot the part that pushed the plane off the ship, the planes have to be pushed back.

"Pushes" isn't the right word. It's like a sling shot.

Our crew would be crouched down in the catwalk, awaiting this kind of problem. When we got the call, we scurried onto the deck, positioned ourselves in front of the wings, and pushed.

On my first time, I was the first one up. (Gung ho!) The plane was a Banshee, which had engines on both sides of the fuselage. As each one started, I felt myself being pushed closer to the engine closest to me! I planted my feet and gave a heave away. Scary.

When the squadron was airborne, we were finished until they returned. Or so I thought. Right back to the chipping, scrapping, and painting.

Let me pause here for a minute to let you know exactly how I felt at that time. *There is no way in the world I was going to do this for the duration of my enlistment!*

Shall I continue, or do I sound like a Wuss? (I looked up the word. It became popular in late 60s. See the things you learn when you write a book?)

Fate had a hand in my life, and not the last time.

We had to take the scrappers to the machine shop to be sharpened on a grinder. Thanks to my dad, who was a tool and die maker, and me having a job in a small shop and the work at the Willow Grove Airfield, I was experienced enough and confident enough to try to get a transfer to the machine shop.

Which I did, with a catch from my previous division.

Every division sends a man or two to perform mess cooking duties (Not considered punishment. Bull!) Since I still was assigned to them, they sent me.

No problem, I thought. *In a few weeks, the transfer will go through, and I'll be working in the machine shop.*

You had to move to a special compartment. The hours were—up at 5 a.m. and finished after the last meal was served. Usually, chow hall was cleaned up at 8 p.m. Back to the compartment. Wash up and hit the sack. Five a.m. comes fast.

The duties were repetitive. Set up the folding tables and benches and, as the crew was eating, we went with a petty officer to replenish our stores. Flour for the bakers. Potatoes, monster cans of vegetables, etc.

On one of these outings, I got into the confrontation I told you about, the squabble that landed me in solitary on bread and water.

One of the worst duties in mess cooking was disposing of the food left on the trays, after they banged them on the insides of large, 50-gallon drums.

There were three other drums with a sailor behind each of them.

They placed the empty trays in the drum of the first guy, who brushed of the residue. Then to the next guy, who did the same. And then to the last guy, who would collect them a few at a time, (They were heavy, made of steel.) and put them on a steam conveyor to sanitize them.

Now comes the fun part—emptying the drum with the remains of the meal.

It had to be brought up on deck, and then to the fantail, to dump it over aft of the ship.

Woe be to you, if you were behind the drum, as you went up the ladder. Especially if they served spaghetti and red sauce.

You dump it after permission is given via loud speaker. "Now hear this. Clean sweep down fore and aft. The fantail is opened for the dumping of garbage."

Over it goes.

Machine shop, here I come, I told myself. *Just a couple more weeks.*

MY FINAL SALUTE

⚓ ⚓ ⚓

I call this, "My Last Liberty Pass." But I ain't coming back!

When I returned to the ship after a whirlwind week of getting married to my dear Bobbie, traveling on a bus to Brooklyn, spending Christmas at home, and then heading back to the ship, I received great news! I was to be leaving the ship January 4th, instead of March. The reason being, the Midway would be shipping out, and my enlistment would be over while out at sea.

They couldn't have that, so they cut me loose!

I was really happy, and so were most of my shipmates—all except one. His name was Donnely, and I think he lived in Connecticut. (I'm glad I didn't know his exact address.) I really never got along with him.

We were the same rank when I left. When I returned, results of a test had bumped him up a rank.

On this day, he was feeling his oats. (I really don't know how it all started.) Seems he didn't like me calling him a SHMUCK, when we were the same rank.

So, I said, "What do you want to do about it, SHMUCK?"

He suggested we go down to our compartment. (I should have smelled a rat.)

We went at it, and I had him in a good headlock, with him hurting.

Someone grabbed me and pinned my arms, a friend of his named Reber. He pulled me down.

Donnely stood over me saying, "You Guinea!"

Did he say New Guinea? I thought. *My family's not from New Guinea.*

Oh, I get it!

Donnely threw a punch and caught me on the side of my face. I shrugged free, and "the hero" ran up the ladder.

I grabbed a spanner wrench and went after him, bloody nose and all.

My good buddy, Reginald Benedict Lewis, grabbed me and brought me to my senses, saying, "If you hit him with that, you'll either get a Bad Conduct discharge and or possibly Leavenworth."

Within a day, I had packed and was off the ship.

As I turned toward it, I gave it the "Italian Salute."

Till this day, I wish I would have caught up to that cowardly bastard.

WAKE UP TO THE REAL WORLD

On November 8, 1952, a young man, Arnold Schuster, was murdered—shot to death while walking to his home in Brooklyn.

I don't know how many murders were committed in the city up to that time, but this was unique.

The young man was targeted on the order of the crime boss of Brooklyn's waterfront. The gangster's sick reasoning was that this young man happened to recognize a notorious bank robber, known to every cop in the city.

Schuster told what he saw to a couple of uniformed cops who, after confronting the guy who was pointed out to them, weren't sure and supposedly kept an eye on him.

They talked to a detective, who approached the guy. The suspect laughed and said, "That happens to me all the time."

The detective took him to the station house, where he was

positively identified, and he admitted to being Willie Sutton!

It became headline news in all the papers. Commenda-tions and promotions were given to the uniformed cops and to the detective. There were interviews, photos taken, and everything printed in all the local papers.
A feather in the cap of New York's Finest.
Not a mention of Arnold Schuster.
Sutton was arrested February 19, 1952.

In the span of two weeks, intimates of Schuster knew of his deed. His family, no doubt, and probably the whole neighborhood knew.
You can imagine him being bombarded by everyone. "But you found him! You should get the credit! And, who knows, there may be a big reward."
That kind of pressure brought Schuster to some attorneys, and the newspapers got ahold of it.
The crime boss dispatched a killer to send a message to others.
The actual murderer of Arnold Schuster was known.

After the death of Schuster, his killer was never seen alive again.

Jump ahead a few years. While waiting to be called, I got into a conversation with an uncle of mine, who was very familiar with how the waterfront worked.
He knew I was going on the force and started giving me advice, his opinions on how things worked in the "real world," which, he said, I was about to enter.
I thought I was already in the "real world." I was married to a gorgeous young lady, had two beautiful kids, had served in the navy, and I'd lived my preteen years right on the same street where my uncle had spent all of his life.
"I'll give you an example," my uncle told me. "You know

that kid who got killed, the one who ratted on Willie Sutton? He got what he deserved."

I was trying to digest what he'd said, and it hit me how naive I was. Crap that I did with my friends, years ago, seemed like, and really was just like, the things he'd described. Kid stuff.

He continued talking.

It bothered me, but I wouldn't give him an argument.

As I progressed in my life, joining the force, etc., I ran into that kind of thinking. Only then, I gave them an argument.

I paid for it by losing a choice assignment, getting lousy assignments, and being scrutinized closely by supervisors. Especially on late tours or during inclement weather.

In each rank I attained I was brought up on charges.

As a patrolman, I deserved it.

As a sergeant, no, and I was found not guilty.

As a lieutenant it was a tie. I thought I wasn't; they said I was. The price I paid was to spend my last five years of a 30-year career in the 28 Precinct in Harlem.

They thought they were punishing me, but it was the best precinct I ever worked in!

The men of the 28 have a saying: "Who's better than the 28? No effing body!"

Did I learn my lesson?

Not yet!

FROM FATHER TO NYPD

Mr. and Mrs. Bello knew I'd applied for the police. They wished me the best and encouraged Barbara and me to stay as long as we liked.

Both of our children were born while we lived in that basement apartment. We stayed there until the time when we had to register the kids in school.

During that period of waiting, I was doing outdoor work, either roofing or putting up tile. Barbara was getting ready to become a mother.

One January morning, when it was still dark, she woke me up.

I didn't know what time it was.

She was already dressed. I was puzzled.

She said, "I'm ready to have the baby."

Total panic!

I sat on the end of the bed, putting on the same clothes I'd had on before I'd gone to bed.

She said, "We have time."

I finished dressing, and we were on the way to Coney Island Hospital.

When we went arrived, a nurse took Barbara behind some doors.

I found a place to sit and was going to wait. (Isn't that what they do in the movies?)

The nurse came out and told me, "You might as well go home. It'll be hours before she gives birth."

I wondered, *Should I do what they do in the movies and wait? Or should I go home?*

I went home.

I slept for a while and then went back to the hospital.

I should have waited. Our daughter Florence Lynn Cocalas entered this world at 8:25 a.m. on January 15, 1955. I went up and saw the baby, and my Barbara.

For the life of me I can't remember with clarity about the birth of my son, James Anthony. He was born April 23, 1956. I only remember going up to the same ward where Barbara was last time she gave birth. She was holding the baby, and she and a nurse were putting a knitted blue outfit on him. We brought him to meet his sister.

It was at this time, the spring of 1956, that I was determined to pass the test for the New York City's police department.

I attended the Delehanty Institute in the city. I went to classes, ran on a track that they had on the roof, and drove home. I don't remember how long I attended their classes, but it did me good.

I passed the written test. Then I waited to be called for the medical.

I was concerned about passing the eye examination.

They put us in a room to fill out some forms and, lo and behold, there on the wall was the eye chart.

I passed the eye test.

Within a couple of weeks, I got a notice in the mail to

report to Van Cortland Park for the physical test.

On that day I had difficulty finding it When I got there, I checked in, and they said, "You're next."

I had to do a broad jump so many feet—no time to stretch or warm up. Straight from my car right to the first test!

I did it, but I strained a muscle in my right leg. Oh no!

While the other guys were doing the broad jump, I was massaging my leg.

I saw the instructor watching me. "You all right?" he asked. "Yeah."

The next test was to lie flat on your back, arms extended out flat, and you had to pick up a certain weight with your shoulder flat on the ground and lift the weight straight up.

It ain't easy.

Next, while lying flat, you got the signal to get up, run to a six-foot high wall, and climb over it.

You continued on to an eight-foot wall, scrambled over that, and hurried on to a tunnel-like pipe and duck-walked through it. It was probably 25 feet long.

Once out, you ran to the finish line. They timed you.

"We'll let you know how you did," they told me.

I knew I did good.

Before I left I saw a husky, tall, redheaded guy struggling to get over a wall that was eight feet high. I hoped he'd make it.

Within a couple of weeks, I got my list number. It was pretty high. I was sure I'd be in the next test, probably by Thanksgiving.

Then the bad news came. I wasn't going anywhere until I explained to the Department of Personnel why I was arrested when I was 15. The next class was in November.

I didn't make that one, but I made the next one, March 16, 1957!

FIRST FIVE DAYS AS A ROOKIE

O n March 16, 1957, I was 25, Barbara was 22, my daughter was two and my son was one. Together, we began a 30-year journey in the New York City Police Department.

I may have worn the uniform, but they were there to share the pain and the loss of holidays together. There were complete days when I didn't see them due to shift hours. There were tours when I left while they were in bed and, when I returned in the morning, they were at school.

And the whole time—visions and memories of my wife ironing my uniforms and years later, her sewing on sergeant stripes. Later still, her attending the promotion ceremony for new lieutenants.

I got the notification to report to 7 Hubert Street in Manhattan, the academy at that time. I have a notation in an old memo book for me to report at 11 a.m., June 28, for graduation ceremonies.

From March 16 to June 28, we attended classes at Hubert Street, physical training at Flushing Meadows, and once, physical training at an armory at Bedford Avenue in Brooklyn. On that day, we were told, "Bring work gloves 'cause we're going to do exercises, including pushups, and it has a wooden floor with splinters."

When I got home that day, I told Bobbie, "I've gotta get some work gloves."

Some of the recruits said, "Go to Battleship Max on Flatbush Avenue, near Avenue U. Show him the shield. He'll give you a discount."

Huh?

I went into the store, picked out a pair, walked to the register, and the owner said, "Let's see your shield."

Huh?

It seems other recruits had been in earlier.

I showed the shield, and he gave me a discount.

At that ceremony at Hunter College we lined up by name in the aisle. When called, you went up, plunked down 10 cents for the pin and got your shield. (I'll bet no one ever told you about that 10 cents. Next time you talk to an old-time cop, ask him.)

My shield # 21742 stayed with me until I made sergeant.

I was told, "Report to the 14th Precinct on West 30th Street, Manhattan, on June 29, at 8 a.m."

Bobbie was at my mom's, waiting with the kids to see me in uniform complete with white gloves. The Dunphy kids came over, as did Detective Johnny Meyers, another neighbor.

"Congratulations Jim," he said. "Where you going? What precinct did they give you?"

I told him, "The 14 Precinct."

(I'm sure I saw steam coming out of his ears and his face was getting a pinkish tinge to it.)

"What?! You kidding me?! You must have some Rabbi!"

In the next few minutes, I learned several things. Number One: "Rabbi" was the same as a hook—a person who can control destinies within the department. Number Two: I was lucky I wasn't going to Harlem, Bedsty, or any other black areas. (*His* words not mine.) Number Three: The area had good eating places.

He continued, "You got the flower market, furrier district, the garment center, Times Square. You sure you don't have a Rabbi? You can tell me. I won't tell anybody. Jeez, you got the Met there, too!"

Det. Meyers was a legend in certain parts of Brooklyn. When he found out I was going in the department he gave me some books to read. It showed victims of gunshot wounds, stabbings and some of autopsies. I thought, *That ain't for me.*

That conversation I'd had with my uncle, regarding "the real world," comes to mind.

I think I showed up at the 14 Precinct on 7:30 a.m. for an 8 to 4 shift. We went through the ritual of lining up before the desk, and a lieutenant turned us out.

My post was between 10th Avenue and 11th Avenue, and Dyer Avenue, an exit for the Lincoln Tunnel. Boring.

The sergeant came around to sign my memo book.

I shouldn't tell you this, but an out-of-town car pulled up and asked how to get to the Empire State Building. I probably gave him the wrong directions.

Tour over. I returned to the station house, signed out and went home.

The next day, a Sunday, I was assigned to Fifth Avenue. I made my 10 o'clock ring.

The sergeant on the switchboard said, "Go to Fifth Avenue

and 30 Street and take care of the problem." He hung up.

The problem was a drunken cop in full uniform, sitting at the curb!

I pulled him up and managed to get him into a building on West 30. I took him to the custodian's room, took off his gun belt, called the station, and told the sergeant, "Have a car meet me at Fifth Avenue and West 30 Street."

I gave them the gun belt.

Welcome to the police department.

The next day was a Monday, and the earth opened up and thousands of people streamed out of the subways. My post was Greeley Square Park, between Broadway and Sixth Avenue. I stayed out of the way of the hordes.

WHAM! An auto accident right by the park!

I stood there, watching, until I realized I was supposed to do something. Embarrassing.

On July 2, a Tuesday, I was involved with something that stayed with me for a long time and affected my approach to serving people. Isn't that what was said on posters in the station houses?

My post was Broadway between West 34 and West 30. I saw an ambulance in front of the Hotel Clinton, a not-so-nice hotel.

My meal hour was coming up in a while. I wondered if I should I go check it out or ignore it. Technically, it was part of my post.

We didn't have radios, and my next scheduled ring was noon, when I would let the station house know I was going to meal.

Ah, what the heck, I thought. *I'll take a walk up there and see what's going on.*

I walked into the lobby and asked the clerk, "Where did the guys from the ambulance go?"

They told me which floor, so I took the elevator up.

I got out and saw a group of people in front of a door,

having a heated discussion.

"I ain't going in there!"

"Me neither!"

"He's got to go in the ambulance!"

I saw another police officer, standing by, observing.

A lady had some papers in her hand, but no one was paying her any attention.

She turned out to be a social worker. The document she was holding was an order from doctor, for the 78-year-old man in the room to be hospitalized for psychiatric evaluation.

I peeked into the room.

Lying naked on a bare mattress stained with urine, feces and with roaches scurrying across his body, wide-eyed and moaning, was the man they were supposed to transport.

I was stunned.

In the hall, no one was moving. No one would touch him! Not the cop, not the ambulance people, not the hotel workers, nor the social worker.

It was an impasse.

Sitting in the hall, was a wheelchair that had been brought up by the ambulance people.

"Give me a sheet," I told the hotel worker. "Bring that wheelchair in the room."

I spread the sheet over the poor man's body.

The bed was on casters, and when I picked him up, it rolled a little.

Under the bed, I saw a woman, lying in her own feces and urine with vermin on her!

I got the man in the wheelchair and yelled at the ambulance people to bring up a stretcher.

The cop was still there, watching, as were the others. I told him, "Give me another sheet."

I covered her and put her on the stretcher. Later, I found out that she regularly came to the room to attend him. But one day, while doing so, she had fallen. When she'd tried to get up, the bed had rolled over her.

She didn't know how long she had been under the bed.

I sat with them both in the ambulance as we went to Bellevue. They were holding hands.

I had five days on the job then.

SHOO FLY

I was getting into the routine of different shifts. Couldn't say the same for my wife. I liked the 4 p.m. to midnight. You didn't have to get up with an alarm, and when I got home about 1 or 1:30, Barbara would be up, and we'd have some tea. I'd check on the children and sometime just sat there and stare at them and realize how blessed we were.

The midnights to 8 a.m. were tough on Barbara. I'd leave about 10:30 p.m. and, if I didn't make an arrest, would be home at 9:30 a.m.

I didn't like the 8 a.m. to 4 p.m. shift. I wouldn't take my car, had to get up with the alarm clock, and had to compete for the bathroom with the kids getting dressed to go to school. When I came home, I'd get involved in watching a show and not get enough sleep.

Enough of my crying. God bless all the wives of policemen and the mothers and the fathers and the children of policeman. They suffer in silence.

I was a rookie and so were about fifteen of us in the precinct. We were spread out, tour-wise. Some were doing 4
p.m. to midnight, while others did day tours, and so on.

There was a rash of windows being broken on Broadway,
mostly on the midnight to 8 a.m. tour. They were doing it for
a pair of shoes or some shirts in a display.

The windows were expensive and replacing them hurt the
stores' business. An association of realtors complained, not
to the local precinct, but to the borough, which had jurisdiction over several precincts.

The word was out to the local precinct. Woe be to the
commanding officer, the sergeant on patrol, or the police
officer who had the post if there was another break.

My buddy, Joe Bannano, and I were doing a late tour (12
to 8 a.m.), and we checked the rollcall for our assignments.

Damn! We both had Broadway, the neighborhood where
the windows were being broken. I had from West 36 to West
38. Joe had West 38 to West 41.

We turned out and proceeded to our posts. It was a little
cold, and I told Joe, "Let's get a fast cup of coffee before we
get on post."

I figured the patrol sergeant wouldn't be looking for us so
soon. Surely, he'd grab a cup of his own before supervising
anyone.

What we didn't know, rookies that we were, was that a
lieutenant from the borough was on patrol. He was called,
"the shoo fly."

There was a Central Restaurant on Broadway. We ducked
in, ordered coffee, and sat at the counter, not even taking our
hats off.

I glanced out the window and saw a guy. I knew in my
heart of hearts, *It's the shoo fly*. Civilian top coat, fedora, like
a guy out of central casting.

"Joe, we're dead," I said. "The shoo fly's outside. Let's go."

We asked the counterman, "Is there another way out?"

We took off out the back door.

Joe was hiking fast toward West 41. I started toward West 36.

"Officer!"

I stopped, put on my angelic face, turned around. "Yes, sir?"

"I'm Lieutenant Donleavy. Call your partner."

"Joe!"

He came back.

The lieutenant said, "Give me your memo books."

If he documented his seeing us in the coffee shop, he'd follow up with disciplinary action. We were rookies, and that could have led to termination.

Joe spoke up first. "Sir, I'd appreciate a break. It won't happen again. I'm going to school. I have special hours and—"

Before he could continue, the lieutenant said more sternly, "Give me your memo books."

Joe continued, "And this will hurt my chances for promotion."

I spoke up. "I'm striving to be a detective, sir."

He relented. "Get back on post, and you better do a straight eight out here tonight."

"Thank you, sir."

We didn't have coffee that tour.

As fate would have it, the very next late tour I had a glass post on Broadway again. No coffee that night either.

I used to smoke back then, so I slipped into a doorway and was enjoying a cigarette...ever on the lookout for the sergeant's car.

I heard glass breaking. Not too close.

I started walking north. A radio car whipped onto Broadway, and I saw figures running.

We got all three.

They had broken a window north of my post.

We had them up against another window, and Tommy Stuart, the operator of the car yelled, "That kid's leg is bleeding. Cocalas, get him in the car."

His partner was cuffing the other two.

The sergeant pulled up just as Tommy was driving away.

Later, I found out that he said, "Where's Cocalas?"

They told him I helped with the arrest and was on the way to St. Vincent's with one of the perps.

Whew!

I AIN'T SO TOUGH

I was still a rookie. Probably always would be to some of these old timers. The expression "Dinosaurs" wasn't used in those days. It became popular years later, when the powers-to-be would warn new recruits to not listen to "the old timers."

"They'll corrupt your virgin thoughts on how to police," they said.

Well, those "old timers" came to the rescue one tour I was working.

I was doing a 4 to 12 on Ninth Avenue between West 42 and West 39. Busy post, lots of pedestrian traffic, lots of car traffic.

The Lincoln Tunnel was only a few blocks west.

There was the bus terminal on the west side between West 41 and West 39 and a bar on the corner of West 41 and Ninth Avenue aptly named the "Terminal."

The old timers said it wasn't named after the bus terminal. But it was called, the "Terminal," because a lot of people ended their lives in there.

You were told not to allow anybody loiter in front of that bar.

I left the station house and proceeded to my post and, as I approached West 41, I saw a few people hanging out in front of the bar.

When some saw me, they went inside. They seemed to know the score.

The others—I had to let them know the rules. "Move along. Either go inside or take a walk."

There I was, all 150 pounds of me, putting on a stern face and voice in an attempt to instill the fear of an arrest or a vicious beating with a night stick! (Hoping they'd move.)

They all did...except one guy.

"Move it inside or take a walk," I told him.

"I'm waiting for my wife," he shot back.

"Well, wait for her inside."

He went inside. Whew!

I continued walking the post, crossing the street.

I walked to the end of the post and was on my way back.

I saw the same guy in front of the bar.

As I headed toward him, he went back inside.

What gives with this guy? I was wondering.

I continued to the corner, crossed the street, and I saw him outside the bar again.

What am I going to do with this guy? I was asking myself.

I started to walk across the street, thinking over my options.

But he was making up my mind for me.

He was coming right at me, there in the middle of the street!

Suddenly, someone grabbed the back of my jacket and said, "Don't let him hit me!"

It was his wife!

He was still coming at us and saying to her, "Woman, you almost got me locked up!"

She mumbled, "Sorry," and the both of them went to the corner and turned toward Times Square.

I was glad it was over.

I continued to walk my post, ducking in for a smoke, and keeping an eye out for the sergeant's car.

My meal was coming up, and I decided I'd head over to Manganaros for a sandwich.

Nah, I thought. *There's no place to sit down in there.*

I went to an Italian grocery across the street. They had tables in the back.

I went to the call box and rang in. "Patrolman Cocalas post 39."

I got a nine o'clock meal. It was about five minutes to nine. They told me, "Call back at nine."

I called back at nine.

This restaurant was run by a family and was low key for many years, until some Hollywood types found it, and the place's popularity sky rocketed.

It was run by an elderly Italian woman, who would sit out front and greet you. You'd walk to the back and sit at one of the tables. It was like being home. Very informal.

I ate a sandwich and had a smoke. (You could smoke in restaurants in those days.) And I went back on post.

I started walking toward 42nd.

A block before the Terminal Bar was a small coffee shop that catered mostly to prostitutes. As I was passing by, the owner tapped on the window.

I went inside and found myself right in the middle of three young, black ladies of the night and a white guy sitting on the end of the counter, yelling curses at each other. (Use your imagination.)

I told them to knock it off and for the ladies to leave.

They didn't want to alienate the police, not even a wet-behind-the-ears rookie. (Was it that obvious?) The women started for the door, but not before they let go with a barrage of curse words, mentioning this guy's heritage.

He exploded off the stool, raging, and determined to get at them.

I tried to stop him.

He shrugged me off.

There went my hat.

I got him in the infamous choke hold. He was strong!

Somebody must have got hold of the cop on the next post. He came in and smacked the guy in the head with his nightstick. The guy went down on all fours.

What was running through my mind was, *It's my post. So, it's going to be my collar, even though I didn't use the stick on him.*

Our friend on the floor was trying to get up.

I'd better cuff him! I thought.

I managed to get the one cuff on, and he was up!

I hung on to the dangling cuff, and he took me for a ride on his back the whole length of the counter, bleeding on my uniform and some on my hands.

In burst the cavalry!

They rushed in and, thinking the blood on me was mine, they pummeled the poor guy.

They dragged him out to a radio car and *put him in the trunk!*

Sorry if I offended anyone, but that's the way it was in those days.

They took him to a hospital.

The next time I saw him was the following day, when they brought him out of a holding cell to appear before the judge.

He had his head bandaged.

Believe or not, he explained to the judge what happened, and when the judge questioned me, I sort of verified what he'd said.

He was released, and I met him outside and told him to wait for his bus in the bus terminal.

Poor guy was on his way home from an out-of-state job he'd just finished.

I doubt he came back to the city any time soon.

OPEN HEART SURGERY

I was doing a day tour, an 8 to 4. I had a post on West 34 from Broadway to Fifth Avenue. The Empire State Building was on West 34 and Fifth. Macy's sat diagonally across from the McCalpin Hotel.

It's a busy intersection because Sixth Avenue (Avenue of the Americas now) going north and Broadway going south meet at West 34.

One day, I saw the sector car pull up to the hotel. It was my post, so I hustled over there.

I recognized the two cops and followed them into the lobby.

They were going into the elevator. I got in.

"What do you have?" I asked them.

They looked at me like I had two heads.

"It's my post!" I told them.

"An aided case," one of them said.

The McAlpin had a pool, as I recall, on the top floor.

This particular day, a group of Jewish doctors had reserved it. They probably reserved it monthly.

We got out of the elevator and saw a group of nude men clustered around a naked guy on the floor. (Apparently, with this particular gathering, swimwear was optional.)

It looked like they were administering artificial respiration to him.

Suddenly, one of them jumped up, left the area, then returned almost immediately.

He leaned over, cut open the left side of the man's chest cavity, shoved his hand inside and started massaging his heart!

There is nothing I can add to that.

The two cops from the sector headed for the elevator and told me, "You got it, kid." And they left.

Normally, a sergeant would respond to supervise a search of the deceased. But the dead fellow was naked. No need.

The poor guy had to be pronounced dead before removal. There were at least 15 physicians there, not to mention the fact that his chest was wide open and his non-beating heart was visible—so we could disregard that formality.

I was advised by the doctors there that they would make arrangements for his removal, because of certain requirements of his religion.

Truthfully, I didn't know the proper procedure, so I went with their suggestions and left. I was relieved.

I didn't have to do a formal identification the next day, and I was glad of that, too. Identifying a body could be more difficult than it needed to be, thanks to the sick humor of some of the morgue personnel.

The rule was: The first officer on the scene of a deceased person must go to the morgue at Bellevue the following day to identify the body.

They just pulled out a slab with a corpse on it, and if it was the body you had seen the previous day, you pronounced it.

Might seem easy, but....

In the area that holds the bodies in slide out drawers, the personnel would determine if you were a rookie.

If they thought you were, they'd pull out a drawer (with a different body) and say, "Is that it?"

The rookie would say, "No."

They'd pull out another drawer. (Again, deliberately displaying the wrong body.)

"Is that it?"

"No."

After a while, they'd show you the right one and say, "Is that it?"

If you weren't a rookie and knew their game, you'd say, "No."

"WHAT?"

They tried it on me once.

In Penn Station the custodians had a locker room with a toilet. There was access to it, if you knew your way around, and the derelicts did. They would sneak in at night and use the toilet.

Probably after complaining to no avail, some heartless individual threw gasoline on one of them, as he was using the toilet, and set him on fire.

(Yeah, I know. Horrible.)

I was called off post to go investigate and report.

The ambulance was there, as was the morgue wagon.

Terrible sight.

Well, as first on the scene, I was required to go to the morgue to let them know, "Yes, that that's the body I saw yesterday at Penn Station."

Mind you, this was the *only* badly burned body in the morgue.

They brought me into the room with the slabs and pulled out the drawer.

They asked, "Is that it?"

"No."

"WHAT!?"

ENDANGERED BABY

Sometime in the '60s, they added another sector in the pre-cinct, running from Fifth Avenue to Seventh Avenue and from West 32 to West 36.

It required eight men to fill the seat. (Two on duty from 4 p.m. to midnight. Two more for the midnight to 8 a.m. Two for the 8 a.m. to 4 p.m. And two off duty.) And yes, I was picked. Yahoo!

My partner was Bob Mullany. He was a veteran in the police department and a World War II veteran, having served in the Marine Corps.

We got along fine. He was the water when I was the fire in some jobs we handled.

There were incidents where he had a calming effect with his approach. If there was a dispute between individuals, he never took sides and, usually, everyone left satisfied.

There was an incident when my actions could have cost the life of an infant. Let me explain:

We received a call of a distraught mother threatening to hurt her child. The neighbors were talking to her through the closed door.

I charged up to the second floor. Bob walked up.

I thought we should kick in the door. He quietly spoke to the neighbors.

He tried talking to the mother, but all he got was, "Leave me alone, all of you!"

The neighbors had damaged the door in an attempt to get in, before we'd arrived.

Bob peeked through a crack in the panel above the security rod that most people put up, making it almost impossible to kick the door in.

He saw that this poor, deranged woman had a baby by its arm. She was holding a broken glass bottle in her other hand, while threatening to cut the child's wrist.

She screamed again, "Leave me alone!"

I took one of the neighbors aside and found out that all the apartments were alike.

I whispered to Bob that I was going up to the unit above and would use the fire escape to get into her apartment.

I prayed that her window wasn't locked.

It wasn't.

I opened the window and came face to face with something I'd feared all my life, a dog! Instinctively, I kicked out and caught it under its chin. It was a combination of pain and shock that sent it to another room.

I peeked into the kitchen.

Should I rush her? I wondered.

Too late. She'd seen me and was raising the child by its arm.

"Okay, okay," I told her. "I'm going. I'm going!"

I walked to the door, motioning with both hands for her to calm down. I removed the security bar and opened the door.

Bob caught my eye signal and slammed the door with his shoulder.

She stumbled.

I grabbed the baby. The woman fell to the floor.

I handed the child to a neighbor and helped Bob cuff the mother. She was crying.

The hallway was crowded with ambulance attendants, other cops, our sergeant, and half of the people who lived in the building.

Our job was over.

The mother went to Bellevue with another cop escorting her. The baby was taken by someone from social service.

Bob and I went for a cup of coffee.

That was the side of Bob that most people knew. There was another side of him very few people saw—decisive and quick to take action.

One such incident comes to mind....

We received a call of an ambulance requested. No further info. We got out of the car and went into the building. We rode an elevator up to the floor given and walked to the door.

We entered and, in an instant, Bob ran to a guy whose wrist had blood pouring from it. His hand was at an odd angle. Others were working on him, holding a rag on his wrist.

Bob muscled in. Tightening the rag, he yelled to me, "Let's go!"

We hustled the man to the elevator. Thankfully, it was still on that floor.

We got him down to the car, Bob holding and tightening the rag. I notified St. Vincent's Hospital to be prepared for us. We got there and turned him over to the staff.

God bless them all.

When we got back in the car, all Bob said was, "The guy's hand was almost off."

God bless Bob.

THREE NYPD DEATHS

We were on a detail out of a precinct that required more security than a single precinct could provide. Some of those assignments were fun like the Macy's Parade, and some not so much fun like the Caribbean Day Parade in Brooklyn.

Sometimes, you'd be out of your element. Different bosses, unfamiliar areas, irregular meal times and locations where you could eat. And when you found out it was for some dignitaries, your discomfort multiplied.

On this day, it was raining. I mean raining! The raincoats were not doing the job. Most of us were looking for a door-way we could duck into to grab a smoke.

Most of us couldn't see or care less about who we were supposed to be guarding.

When we were dismissed, some would have to go back to their precincts to finish a tour, and others, like the guys from my precinct, were released for the day.

We grabbed a subway back, and most went in to change.

I didn't. I told the guys, "I got my car, and I'm going to Brooklyn."

Guys piled in, six in all, still in the wet raincoats. I put the vent on, so I could see and not total the car on the bridge.

When we over the Brooklyn Bridge, guys stated sounding off—

"Jim, could you drop me off at the next corner?" and so on until there was only Vinnie, sitting next to me in the front seat.

He hadn't moved when guys from the back of the car had scrambled over him to get out. Probably too tired, wet, and miserable to bother.

Vinnie lived south of me. It was a little out of my way. No problem.

As we were going south on Third Avenue, a radio car pulled up to us at a light. I rolled the window down, so he could see I was on the job.

He looked at me, then leaned forward to check out Vinnie.

I turned, looked at Vinnie, still in the center of the seat, and said, "Vinnie, shove over."

The cop shook his head and drove off.

After a second, we laughed. We knew what the cop must have been thinking.

On February 14, 1963, St. Valentine's Day, Police Officer Vincent Zichettella, Shield 13734, was shot to death.

On February 15, 1963, I was doing an 8 a.m. to 4 p.m. and driving into work. I heard on the radio that a police officer was shot at Penn Station.

I thought I heard them say Zichettella! Yeah, they said it!

"Policeman Vincent Zichettella was shot in Penn Station!"

When I walked into the station house the lieutenant on the desk called me over. "You hear about what happened?" he asked me.

"Just heard it on the radio."

"You knew him, so they picked you to be at his wake. They'll let you know when."

I was there, in uniform, white gloves and all, standing at the front of the coffin.

The family was no more than five feet from me.

When they came to kneel at the coffin, I said to myself, *This is not right. People need more space at a moment like this.* So, I left and stood at the entrance instead.

There had been a series of stickups of Loft candy shops in Midtown. Vinnie was working a day tour on West 34 between Seventh and Eighth Avenues.

He must have been aware of a stickup. People saw him running after someone through an arcade that goes from West 34 to West 33. The guy jumped into a cab.

Vinnie caught up with the vehicle on Penn Station's taxi ramp that goes into Eighth Avenue. When Vinnie opened the cab's door, he was mortally shot in the face.

The taxi took off but was stopped Uptown. After a shootout, the perp was arrested.

Did Vinnie's death affect me personally?

I learn from every experience. Not so much emotionally, but tactically. I'll give you an example.

Upon promotion to sergeant, they used to assign you to a precinct for a period of six months to get your feet wet, so to speak. You learned how to turn out the platoon, how to act when called to a scene, how to exert authority, etc.

Then they transferred you to your permanent command.

We had a young sergeant assigned to the 14 Precinct. He did his six months and was sent to the precinct that handles the Bowery. He, his driver, and probably the sector car team assigned to the location, confronted a man with a knife.

The man lunged forward. He was shot six times and still managed to stab Sergeant Edward J. Johnson to death.

Later, I had a situation, confronting a man with a knife, and

I knew not to get close. I'll tell you about that sometime.

Vinnie, I knew personally.

Sergeant Johnson I got to know professionally, while driving him one tour, just prior to him being transferred.

The only contact I ever had with Detective Anthony Campisi was on November 4, 1966.

I was partnered up with one of the best human beings I ever knew, Tommy Stuart. We received a call of someone lying in the street at West 38 and Sixth Avenue.

We got out and observed a white male—definitely not a bum—lying in the street with a blood stain on his clothes. The ambulance from St Clare's Hospital was just pulling up.

Tommy got closer, and he spotted a police shield hanging from his neck.

He says, "Jim, this guy's a cop."

The attendants on the ambulance were known to me and Tommy, and they hustled out the stretcher, put him on it and loaded him into the ambulance. I jumped in.

We got to the hospital and rushed him inside.

I tagged along as they stripped him down.

I remember how white his skin was.

I'd never heard the expression, "bled out," until then.

God forgive me for even thinking this at a time like that, but I noticed that his underwear was clean. And I remembered what my mom used to say about that: "Suppose you got in an accident...."

Detective Campisi had been assigned to Public Morals and was effecting the arrest of a female. As they left the St. Claire Hotel, her pimp came up behind the detective and stabbed him in the side, probably puncturing his heart.

The pimp and the prostitute were both arrested. He served 30 years and was paroled. She was acquitted.

THREE HORRIBLE SIGHTS IN ONE TOUR

If you've been to Manhattan during working hours, actually any time, you know that walking in the city is a chore. Now picture driving a car there for eight hours. Now, imagine driving a vehicle during the winter there with the rain and the snow, or in the heat of summer with no air conditioning.

You've got the windows down, and you pull up alongside a bus, whose exhaust is blowing in your window, and the light turns red, and you're stuck there until it turns green.

But there are aspects of being driving around the city in a patrol car that can be worse than snow, heat, or bus exhaust. Much, much worse....

"Come on, Bob," I told my partner one day. "Let's get out of here and go on 11th or 12th and get some air."

As we left our sector (a no-no), we got waved down by some worker on 10th Avenue.

We pulled over, and he told us, "A guy got hit by a truck up the street!"

We drove up 10ᵗʰ Avenue a couple of blocks and saw a group, gathered around the victim. We got out.

A truck had backed into a spot as a young man in his 40s and his father were walking between two trucks. Somehow, the older man had either slipped or was clipped by the truck. He'd fallen beneath the rear tire.

I hate even writing this. The poor guy's head had been crushed.

The son was hysterical. We tried to distract the son by physically blocked his view.

The sector car assigned to the radio run pulled up, and they could see what had happened. We let them know we were waved down.

"No sweat," they said. "We got it."

We stuck around until the ambulance showed.

We were glad to get out of there.

On the way back to our sector, at Ninth Avenue and West 34, we saw what looked like an accident. Traffic was backing up.

I got out of the car and walked to the intersection.

People were screaming.

What I saw has been with me all my life.

Two young ladies had been walking with others across Ninth Avenue. A truck had knocked both women down and rolled over them with front and rear wheels.

I knew they were dead and did something I shouldn't do, but I had to. I took out two blankets and completed covered them.

Other emergency units were responding. Some detectives showed up and took the driver into a restaurant.

I walked back toward the truck and on the front bumper was a perfect imprint of lips with purple lipstick.

How do you forget those things?

We couldn't contribute anything to the investigation. We stuck around until we were relieved by another unit.

What do you do with those images?

Do you go home and tell your dear wife what you saw that day?

No. You store it away and continue doing the job until it's all filled up.

Then what?

COPS STAMPEDE ON 42 STREET

One of the areas we tried to avoid was 11th Avenue between West 42 and West 40.

Prior to the restricting of the slaughter houses in the city there were two, back to back, on 11th Avenue. (I looked up the info on the computer. Do you know what they called slaughterhouses in the old days? "Abattoir.")

Until 1930, there was a tunnel under the streets to move cattle to the abattoir. (I like using that word.) I believe they did that because, when the cattle used the streets, they were causing traffic problems.

I don't know the year they closed them, but I remember coming back from Pennsylvania in the late forties and exiting the Lincoln Tunnel. That odor was sickening.

We picked up the job when all other units weren't available. It wasn't our sector. We knew about the stink!

We were told by the foreman of a demolition team that

they were about finished tearing down one of the buildings, and when they entered the second one, they found a body.

He wouldn't go in but told us it was on the lower lever, floating in water.

What?!

We ventured in and, sure enough, there was a body floating in water about ten feet below us. Needless to say, it stunk.

That wasn't a job for guys like us. We called for emergency service and the sergeant, and told Central, "We may need the detective squad." It sure wasn't a natural death.

We went outside in the air to wait.

It still reeked, even from out there.

I noticed, if you looked inside, while standing in the sun, you couldn't see more than ten feet into the darkness. The emergency squad showed, as did the sergeant. They decided they had to send one of their guys down into the water.

When the detectives came, they talked to the foreman and decided that a derelict had somehow gotten in, wandered around in the dark, and fell into this opening.

As for the water, it was probably from rain that had come through the holes in the roof and flowed downward, picking up who knows what and washing it down into that hole.

I didn't envy the cop, putting his waders on, preparing to be lowered into that hole. They had an emergency light on him.

While attempting to put a line on the body, he stirred up some putrid water. They needed help pulling him up.

"Cocalas, Mullany," somebody said, "Give those guys a hand."

A couple of guys from emergency, Bob, and I took hold of the line. (Guess who was first on the line. Guess who was second. Lucky us.)

We started to pull, and the body got caught on some rough cement edges of the hole.

We pulled, hard, and we tore his body.

Yes, tore it. He literally started coming apart! The smell

made me nauseous, and my hat was coming off.

I reached for my hat and let go of the line, as did Bob. The body, or I should say, *parts* of the disintegrating body, were falling and splashing into the water below.

Bob and the detective and the sergeant and I all started running to the street to get some fresh air.

Remember I said you couldn't see more than ten feet inside the building?

Well, here came a bunch of cops pouring out of the dark, charging toward some workers, who were standing around, trying to see what was going on.

They saw us, got scared, and started running, too. So, we were all running toward 42 Street.

It couldn't be helped.

The emergency cops were rather annoyed. (I don't want to use the other expression.) They called for another one of their units. It was out of our hands.

The sergeant told us to resume patrol.

Was he kidding? No, he wasn't.

We finished the rest of our tour, stinking like a couple of dead guys.

A GOOD ROBBERY ARREST

I was rummaging thru some old, I mean *old* documents, memo books, letters of commendations, civilian complaints, department charges, disciplinary transfers, arrest records and so much more. Some of it I remember, and a heck of a lot of it, I don't.

Here's one, straight from the felony complaint....

The defendant did violently and feloniously assault deponent with the intent to take his life or to do him grievous bodily harm, and without justification: Deponent (that's me) states that he found the defendant lying on the sidewalk, and as he approached and bent over to help the defendant who had abrasions on his scalp, the defendant jumped up, and struck the officer about the face and chest with his fists and refused to desist. The officer had to use a measure of force to effect the defendant's arrest.

I don't remember this incident. Sorry, one thing I know— he didn't hurt me, but I'm sure as heck that I hurt him.

That happened Nov 1, 1959, in front of 423 Eighth Avenue at 11:30 p.m. I'm guessing that this was in front of a bar. He'd probably gotten his load on, and they'd thrown him out.

How about another one off the pile? (This one I remember.)

So-and-So #1 and So-and-So #2, while acting together and in the company of each other, did violate the provisions of Sect.887 Subd7 of code of criminal procedures in that they were dressed and disguised in a manner calculated in an attempt to not be identified. So-and-So #1 was wearing a ladies' wig, pink ladies' slacks, ladies' shoes with high heels, a woman's purse, and his face made up with rouge and lipstick. Defendant So-and-So #2 wore a ladies' skirt, high heel shoes, earrings, a woman's wig and rouge and lipstick.

Sounds almost laughable. But what's not mentioned was that these two were attempting to rob at gunpoint an individual at 5:45 a.m. at Ninth Avenue and West 36. My partner and I chased the pair and disarmed one of them of a loaded 22.cal revolver.

There you have a little potpourri of what cops on the streets are confronted with.

Just to round it off: We were doing a day tour in our sector and got a report of a holdup at West 33 and Sixth Avenue. We were close.

When we pulled up, the owner of small haberdasher met us at the curb.

"There were three of them!" he yelled, "Young, black. One of them has a gun! They got on the bus!"

We started driving up Sixth Avenue and caught up to the first bus.

"Can't be that one," my partner said. "It's gotta be the one further up!"

We pulled alongside the next one.

"There!" I pointed at the rear of the bus. "They're sitting in the back!"

We drove in front of the bus. It stopped.

We got out of the car and approached the bus. The driver opened the door.

"Don't open the back door!" we told him.

We boarded the bus, weapons out.

Everyone stood up and started moving forward—except the three, young, black kids in the rear. They stayed put.

Under one of their seats was a paper bag with a gun in it and the store's money.

That was easy.

WOOSTER STREET FIRE

In Greeley Square, right across the street from the now defunct Gimbles, was one of the call boxes for the 14 Precinct. And right across from the call box in the lobby of the Martinique Hotel was a coffee shop, which I was about to go into and have a cup of joe (coffee to you.) Right after I made my ring.

I hope you know by now that you were assigned a time to ring every hour and after you made your ring you were to stay by the call box for one minute in case they had an assignment. I really believe it was another way for the sergeant on the switchboard to harass you, as in, "Weren't you told to stand by the call box in case we needed you?"

I had less than a year on the job, and they'd caught me a couple of times. I can see them now, giggling in the station house. I remember thinking, *If I ever make boss I hope I'll remember what it was like to be on the bottom of the ladder.*

Okay. Back to that morning....
I could taste that coffee. I'd make the ring and then relax

for a while.

"Patrolman Cocalas," I said. "Post 26."

I hung up and was starting for the coffee shop. The box phone rang. I muttered, "Stupid S.O.B." I picked it up. "Patrolman Cocalas, post 26."

"Go over to 12th Avenue and pick up a barrier truck and bring it to Wooster Street. They got a big fire there, and some fireman were killed."

Wow!

I thought two things. *Where is Wooster St, and how big is the truck?*

I commandeered a taxi and told the cabbie, "Take me over to 12th."

"What's up?" he asked.

"There's a big fire on Wooster Street. Hey, I gotta take a truck there. How do I get there?"

"Take 12th Avenue down to Houston and take a west bound street."

The guys at the piers were waiting for me. They pointed to a truck and said, "The keys are in it."

It was already running. Thank you, Lord!

I had to back it out. I got it in gear and slowly, I mean *slowly*, backed out onto 12th Avenue.

Grinding the truck's gears into first, off I went.

I never got it out of first.

I arrived at the scene. Total chaos. Poor guys.

A boss yelled, "Back it in there!"

I managed to park it, and the cops assigned to the fire scene started taking the barriers off and putting up a perimeter.

I lingered a bit, then said to myself, *I'd better get out of here before some boss puts me to work!*

There was a cop sitting in a radio car on the edge of the mess. He said, "How's about a ride back to the 14?"

"I just dropped off the truck."
"Hop in."
I thought, *Hey, I'm going to get that coffee after all!*

No, I didn't let anyone know I was back.
I was starting to learn how to play the game.

BODY ON THE TRACKS

Our precinct had the garment center, the flower market, and the furrier district. It had the infamous Times Square, the beautiful Empire State building, the New York Library on Fifth Avenue, the one with the two lions out front, named Patience and Fortitude, (The next time you're on *Jeopardy* you'll know), the historic James A. Farley Post Office, and the hub of transportation, Pennsylvania Station. Thousands use it every day to travel on commuter trains into the city, and when the day's work is done, they rush through it, once again, to catch trains and go home.

We were doing a late tour, a midnight to 8 a.m., when we got a call to report to Penn Station. We were informed that one of the engineers saw a body on the tracks. Gulp!

After shutting off the power, we boarded a diesel-pulled train into the tunnel.

We got onto a walkway and headed into the darkness. The only light we had was from the diesel's single front light. It was eerie. The train was slowly moving forward while we were on the tracks. The damn thing was making a steady chugging sound. The tunnel ahead was completely black.

A little way up, on the side of the tracks, we saw a severed hand.

Emergency Service was with us, and they shoveled it into a body bag.

A bit farther ahead, they found the torso. They put it into the same body bag. I remember it looked scorched.

We didn't see any more remains.

They didn't need us anymore, so we climbed onto the walkway and made our way back to the terminal.

We waited. There was a chance that our boss might have wanted us to search the remains. Fortunately, for us, a couple of jurisdictions were involved and someone else did it. They found ticket stubs and determined the poor guy had boarded the train at 5 p.m.

Somehow, he'd fallen onto the tracks, and thankfully, eventually, an engineer had reported it. But in the hours before that, of all the engineers who had driven through that tunnel, none of them had seen a body.

Can you believe it?

I don't.

FIRE IN THE FURRIER DISTRICT

I was riding with Bill Hall doing a 4 p.m. to midnight. We were on Seventh Avenue at West 28. Just a normal tour so far. That area of Seventh Avenue is part of the furrier district.

From one of the buildings on my left, I saw smoke coming out of third-floor window.

I told Bill, "Call it in, 305 Seventh. I'm going in."

I hopped out of the car, and I was about to enter, when Billy Bombacie called to me, "Wait up."

Billy and John McKeon were on Seventh and saw me get out of the car and hustle into the building. He didn't know about the fire. He just saw a cop in a hurry and thought he could help. Cops are like that.

"There's a fire on the third floor," I said.

In the lobby we saw the elevator operator, Louis Green.

I asked him, "You know you got a fire on the third floor?"

"What?!"

"Take us up!"

When we reached the third floor, we could see smoke coming from beneath a double door entrance. Not a lot.

The operator told us whose office it was.

I was wondering if we should force the door open.

What we did was, to put it tactfully, stupid.

Billy and I each grabbed a handle and pulled.

The doors opened and then real smoke was coming out. (I think people use the expression "billowing." I decided to use that and "harrowing" to describe the scene and the experience when I wrote up the official report.)

Billy was saying, "Let's get out of here!"

Louis was holding the elevator.

I crept in a little. Didn't see any flames.

"Jimmy, let's go!"

"Wait! I hear somebody!"

It sounded like a groan.

I yelled, "Keep that door open!"

I got down and started to crawl.

I found a man, lying there with parts of his upper body— maybe just his clothes—on fire.

"There's a guy in here!" I shouted.

I took of my jacket and smothered the flames on his chest. I started to pull him across the floor. "Billy, give me a hand!"

We had gotten him to the hall by the time the firemen arrived.

They wrapped him in what I found out later were sterile sheets.

We got out of the way and were sitting on the floor, leaning against the wall, trying to catch our breath.

The patrol sergeant showed up and...in that hallway...in front of all those fireman...he said to me, "Button that jacket!"

I cannot write what I really wanted tell him.

Anyway, they removed that burn victim to St. Vincent's Hospital.

He was the owner of a company that sold furs.

Later, his son told us he'd been in the office that day because he was expecting to make a sale.

According to the fire department, he'd been cleaning a fur with some sort of inflammatory liquid and smoking a cigar.

They think the ash fell into the liquid.

After all was said and done, Billy and I were recommended for the Monthly Hero Award, given by *The New York Journal-American*. But it was awarded to a detective who was shot and killed on a train during an attempted mugging.

Would you consider me crass if I admit that, when I heard the news of his death, I actually thought, *Too bad he wasn't on that train the* next *month?* Yeah, I know. Not one of my better moments.

To put an end to this story....

That day, Bill and I went to St. Vincent's to see how our burn patient was doing.

We were met by his son, who said to us, "My father made a sale that day. Did you see his wallet anywhere?"

Bill went ballistic. "How could you say such a thing?! This officer risked his life to save your father!"

The son apologized.

We left.

Oh, yeah. The guy died the next day.

SAFE BURGLAR

Here's an example of a typical situation we encountered in Midtown. Burglary was the crime of choice in the area with many hundreds of lofts, offices, and all sorts of street level stores.

Some had an alarm system with a company called Holmes. When they received an alarm, they would notify Police Headquarters, who would transmit, "Holmes alarm at such-and-such address."

We would respond and, at times, we had to wait for the Holmes people to arrive in order to gain entrance to those large office buildings.

There were keys to these buildings in their main office in Midtown. (I forget the address.) And when they were alerted to a certain location, they were issued keys to enter the building and the office itself. While few arrests were made with this system, they did prevent further loss of merchandise, if the burglars managed to get in. They may have heard the elevators coming up, etc. In any event, as I said before, few actual arrests were made. Except in this case....

Jimmy Conner and I were doing a 4 to midnight in RMP (radio motor patrol) Sector 2 and John O'Hara and Michael Killeen in RMP 792 sector 3 were alerted at 10:20 of a possible burglary in progress at #1 West 39. The maintenance man had reported that he'd heard noise from the seventh-floor offices of Affiliated Publishers.

Jimmy and I positioned ourselves in the stairwell. O'Hara and Killeen went up and approached the door. It had been forced open.

As they stepped inside, they saw figures running to the back stairs. Toward us. One of them tried to muscle past me. Necessary force was used to restrain him.

Two others tried to run back up but stopped when they saw O'Hara and Killeen, guns drawn. They were carrying a briefcase with burglary tools.

That's what cops do besides giving parking tickets.

Those three were on the lower ring of burglars. Bob and I were an 8 a.m. to 4 p.m. tour and on patrol at West 34 and Eighth Avenue. We got a report of a burglary of a finance company (I forget the name.) We were literally right in front of the building.

We entered through the front entrance on Eighth Avenue and climbed the stairs to the second floor. The office to the finance was opened. With care, we entered and saw an overturned safe. A big one.

The guy knew what he was doing. He'd peeled back the metal from the bottom of the safe exposing a concrete base. He'd been preparing to weaken the concrete with acid!

Other officers arrived, including the sergeant and his driver. Plenty of cops, no burglar.

We made a search of the building, checking stairwells and the roof, trying all the doors to the offices.

When we were satisfied, we went down to the office,

where guys were still gaping at the technique the burglar had used.

We were unaccustomed to seeing a safe as big as that turned upside down and the bottomed ripped open. A real pro.

I told my partner, "The guy's gotta be in the building."

I started walking up the stairway. At about the fifth floor, I came face to face with him. Instinctively, I kicked out! I pulled my gun. He knew he was defeated. I marched him down. He said he'd been hiding on the top of the elevator!

At the station house and during the preparation of forms, I asked him about his profession. And he told me he could open most safes.

The next day, while he was being arraigned and in the holding pen, and I was sitting in the front row. They called a case. And this huge guy came up and was standing in front of the big oak table with all the arraignment papers spread across it. As the court officer was reading the charges, this man overturned the table!

Three things happened: One, the judge was a blur going out the side door. Two, the arresting officer grabbed the man around his chest, but was being carried about like a kid riding on his dad's back. And three, I jumped up and got him in a choke hold. I held onto him until other officers carried him into the holding cell and were able to put cuffs on him.

I went back into the court room and found my shield among the papers. I had civilian clothes on and had been wearing it like the detectives you see on television.

While in the holding cell, I saw my guy shaking his head, probably thinking he was glad he wasn't into the rough stuff.

HELICOPTER IN THE HUDSON

It wasn't easy, working in Manhattan as a police officer, whether you were on foot patrol on West 42 on a Saturday night, or at a school crossing during the day, or a bank post until the bank was opened and you were sure no one was being held hostage, (Don't laugh. You had to stay there until 9:30 a.m.) or a post on a midnight to eight, or a fixed post at a premise on strike, or at a hospital guarding someone else's prisoner, or riding in the back of a patrol wagon loaded with prostitutes destined for central booking, or being sent to another precinct for crowd patrol, or guarding a crime scene with a ripe DOA sitting on a toilet, or being ordered by the sergeant to bring the lieutenant on the desk a flute. (No, it wasn't a musical instrument. It was a soda bottle full of whiskey, and no, you didn't refuse.)

And even worse would be having to drive the boss for eight hours, and he didn't smoke! But the toughest were the times when you had to take action, and you couldn't look in a book to find out how to react.

One of those times was at 4:10 p.m., Tuesday, June 25, 1968 at West 30 and the Hudson River.

A helicopter crashed in the Hudson with people on board.

I was at West 30 with P. O. John Gerlich in RMP 1132. We were a block from the piers.

We got there and hopped out of the car. We saw a guy in the water with a five-year-old kid in his arms and some people sitting on the pontoons of the helicopter.

The two of us stripped down, gun belts and all. (I'm only going to relate what I did.) I jumped in the water and swam out to the guy holding the kid. We got close enough to hand the child to people on the pier.

I swam out to the helicopter. Later, there are reports that it was 200 feet from the piers. I don't think it was that far.

The pilot had a gash on his forehead. Not life-threatening, but boy, was he pissed! The others weren't exactly calm, but I think they knew that they would be all right, having seen a bunch of cops enter the water.

As I said, the pilot was pissed and said in no uncertain terms we, meaning me, should have waited for someone with lifesaving devices like a boat or life preservers.

While he was yelling at me, I was holding on to the pontoons, my feet dangling below the helicopter. I felt something metallic under the helicopter and thought, *Suppose my feet get tangled in something down there. If it sinks it'll drag me down!*

I heard more splashing and knew some were jumping into the water, unnecessarily. (If you got wet, you'd be guaranteed recognition, either on the official report or in the papers, whether you did anything useful or not.)

We got everyone off the helicopter and out of the water, but we had a hard time getting one of our own out. We finally did.

It was chaos on the pier. I was putting on my uniform and was told by my sergeant, "Put this blanket on. You're going to be interviewed by television reporters."

I was.

My family said I sounded and looked okay. I never saw it.

We returned to the station, and they forced us to give interviews. The captain of the 14 Precinct recommended department recognitions for all involved and he sent it to the police commissioner. It would be feather in the cap of the precinct.

What we got was—to be invited to the Life Saving Benevolent Association, where we received monetary compensation and a medal and some great pictures of all who were involved.

And you thought we only gave out summons.

SOME THINGS YOU DON'T GET USED TO

Bob Mullany and I were finishing an 8 a.m. to 4 p.m. tour and were approaching West 30 and Seventh Avenue. The station house was on West 30, between Seventh Avenue and Sixth Avenue.

If only we had turned that corner a couple of minutes earlier, I would have double parked the car, the 4 p.m. to midnight would have relieved us, we'd have gone into the station house, saluted the desk, signed out, gone up to the locker room, changed into civilian clothes, proceeded to Penn Station, and caught the train to Laurelton. Home Sweet Home.

But—and it's a big but—we got waved down by a middle-aged man, who was waving his arm and saying something.

Bob told me, "Pull over. Roll down the window."

There was no refusing Bob.

I pulled to the curb and rolled down the window.

"I live on the fourth floor," the man said, "and something smashed onto the roof and caved in my ceiling!"

"Did you find out what it was?" I asked.

"No, I didn't."

I was thinking, *So, what do you want us to do? I've got to catch a train. Couldn't you have waited a few minutes?*

Bob read my mind. "Come on," he said. "Let's see what happened."

There was no arguing with Bob.

We walked up to the guy's apartment to take a look.

Yep, there was a big bow in the ceiling.

I said, "Take us to the roof."

He hesitated. I got the feeling he'd been up there already. He pointed to a staircase.

I went ahead of Bob.

The roof door had a latch on it. It opened with a little push.

There, in the middle of the roof, was the body of a nude woman, lying face down in a depression in the roof!

The guy said, "Oh, my god," and left.

I told Bob, "Take the car back and notify the squad. Tell the lieutenant we'll need a policewoman to search her. She's got a necklace or a chain on her neck. I'll handle this. It'll be a while."

"You sure?" Bob asked.

"Yeah. See you tomorrow."

After a while, the sergeant showed up and sometime later a police woman arrived.

There was no pretense of being used to this type of thing.

The sergeant said, "We'll wait for the squad."

I told the sergeant, "She's got a chain on her neck."

Poor woman. Her face was pressed against the softened roof.

The sergeant said to the policewoman, "When the squad gets here, you'll have to remove the chain.

Meanwhile, the squad was questioning people in the

adjourning hotel. I think it was The Penn. They got her name, etc. and were talking to the sergeant.

The sergeant told the policewoman, "Okay, Officer. Would you get that chain off her?"

In order to do that she had to turn the body a little to unlatch the chain. She tried, but the face was actually imbedded in the roof.

The sergeant said, "Let's wait till the morgue wagon shows up.

They finally arrived.

"All right, Cocalas," the sergeant said. "You can take off."

He didn't have to tell me twice!

W. Eugene Smith

BABY IN DISTRESS

Bob and I were doing an 8 a.m. to 4 p.m. tour in our sector, when a call came over, mentioning that a baby was in distress, and the mother needed assistance. Now, the call wasn't as exact as that, but we got the general idea.

They gave the address and told us an ambulance was on the way.

It was on West 37 between Ninth Avenue and Tenth. It wasn't our sector, but Bob immediately headed toward the address. We were of the same mind. *Get there and help in any way we can.*

As it happened we were the first car there. There were people outside a first-floor apartment. A woman was holding a baby in a blanket. She shoved the child at me and said, "The kid's not breathing right."

Bob told me, "Let's go!"

He ran to the car, opened the door for me.

We took off.

We were really moving!

He notified Central we were on our way to St. Vincent's.

I started to breath gently in the mouth of the baby. I really didn't know if what I was doing was right, but the child was alive when we handed him over at St. Vincent's.

There was a whole bunch of nurses and doctors waiting. God bless them.

We gave them as much info as we had and left.

As we were driving back, Bob said, "What's the matter?"

I was quiet for a while, then I told him, "I did this before with my son, Stephen, who was ten-months-old. He didn't make it."

"Jeez, Jim, I'm sorry."

He didn't ask anymore.

Bob had been around the block, seen combat, worked the job, and who knew what personal experiences he'd had?

So, we sat quiet for a while.

Finally, I started to tell him about W. Eugene Smith, and how he helped me extract photos of Stephen from a 35mm roll of film.

"Wait," Bob said. "I gotta hear this. Let's get some coffee."

Over coffee, I told him....

After my son passed, I realized we had very few photos of him, but I remembered taking moving pictures of him, while we lived in the Bellos' basement apartment.

One day, while I was walking a foot post in the flower market, I stopped in one of the wholesale shops for a smoke. I think it was called the Supreme or Superior.

On one wall were snapshots of cops in uniform getting out of their radio cars, going into the shop empty-handed, and coming out with their arms loaded with flowers. Maybe around Easter.

The snapshots were taken from an apartment across the

street and a few houses down, probably from the third floor. (I could be a detective!)

Anyway, curiosity didn't kill the cat.

I walked across the street, found the right house, and on the third floor I met W. Eugene Smith. A true legend, though I didn't know it then.

His apartment was loaded with cameras and other equipment used in developing stuff.

I noticed he had some scars on his face.

I told him about the pictures in the flower shop. After some small talk, I left.

Jump ahead a few years.

I was, and still am, a buff on WWII, and I saw some pictures that he'd taken. One was of a Marine holding a baby taken from the rubble of some village in the Pacific. I also read that he was wounded in Okinawa by a grenade, hence the scars on his face. (Anybody reading this, look him up on your computer, read about his life, and you'll see why they call him a legend.)

Now, I had no idea of his notoriety at the time of our first meeting, nor when I asked him if it was possible for him to print some photos from the 35mm film I had.

He did.

He has since passed.

Bob and I worked well together. There was one occasion when his compassion came through, and we did the right thing.

We were on a 4 p.m. to midnight and got waved down on West 36 by some guy with his family.

We knew what he was going to say before he said it. "Officer could you help us out?"

He had come into the city to sightsee and to visit the Empire State Building and had parked his car in a lot. He'd been told the lot would close at 11 p.m. It was about 10:45.

This wasn't the first time this had happened at that lot.

He had his wife, son, and daughter with him. He said they lived in Connecticut.

"Do you have another set of keys with you, besides the one you left with the lot?" I asked them.

They did.

Bob and I both had the same idea. "Wait here," we told them.

We went to a Con Ed crew working on Seventh Avenue and borrowed a crowbar from them.

We didn't have to say anything to the guy and his family. He knew what was up. He said, "We'll be on the corner."

In about five minutes, they were headed back home to Connecticut.

Like I said, we did the right thing. We retrieved Con Ed's bar and returned it to them.

POLICE EXPOSURE SHAKES NEW YORK TO VERY CENTER

FOUR SEPARATE SYSTEMS OF GRAFT EACH HEADED BY A HIGH POLICE DEPART- MENT OFFICIAL.

MY FIRST COMPLAINT

How am I going to tell you this and not sound like a cry baby?

These incidents occurred close to fifty years ago. You're about to get one's person view on the machinery within the NYPD. If you read history, you'll see that the department was plagued by scandals involving illegal gambling and payoffs by bookmakers. There were many who lined their pockets and were never caught and others who paid the price. Some lost their jobs. Some, not many, went to jail. Some killed them- selves. And one died in the electric chair in 1915. That would be Lt. Charles Becker. (Look him up.)

In 1942, there were indictments brought against 32 police officers, who took bribes from a gambling syndicate. Anyone remember Harry Gross from Brooklyn or Abe Reles taking a dive out of the Half Moon Hotel at Coney Island? Too far in the past? How about the Knapp Commission in the 1970s, or Serpico, or former detective, William Phillips, tried and convicted of murder, who did over 25 years in prison?

The incident I'm going to write about requires going beyond what was officially put on paper. Here goes....

In the back room of the station house in the 14 Precinct was a board with pictures of known gamblers. That board was covered up with an old-fashioned, roll-down shade to prevent unauthorized people from looking at it.

As in, "Hey! Ain't that So-and-So from 31?"

I've always thought it was for us, so in case we saw any of them, we could get friendly with them. (Am I stretching my imagination? We'll see.)

The sector, who was assigned Ninth Avenue to the Hudson, was driving around and spotted one of the faces on the board.

What to do, what to do?

Whenever the sergeant would instruct you in the back of the station house, he might mention different crime trends, etc. and make a mention of gamblers in your sector and to report them.

Lo and behold, in the jargon of today, "CYA," and they did. (Now put your thinking caps on.) No action could be taken against the two in the sector. It would be too obvious. The report went to the Borough Office. They had to notify the division and the division sent out plainclothesmen to arrest this jerk who was upsetting the apple cart. To show initiative, the CO switched the men from one sector to another.

The men, who were switched to the area where the jerk was first spotted, spotted him again. Not right away.

No, he wasn't in jail. Either he'd paid a fine or had his case pending.

What to do, what to do?

They did what they thought was right. They reported seeing him.

Same scenario. Can't discipline them. Too obvious. They were just doing their job.

Now let's pause here. Remember the child and the mother who was going to cut the kid's wrist? Bob and I didn't identify the baby's name nor the mother's. We heard from personnel in the station house, "The CO knows the mother." We never pursued it any further.

On this particular Sunday, Bob and I were doing an 8 a.m. to 4 p.m. tour. It had been a quiet day so far.

We got a 1002 the house. Bob was driving. We pulled up to the station, and the lieutenant said, "See the captain."

No problem, I thought. *Bob and I haven't had to rough up anybody lately.*

His office was at the head of a winding staircase. He was sitting behind a desk.

"Want to see me, Cap?" I asked.

Without looking up, he said, "Get me a danish and coffee and the *New York Times*." (You didn't think he was going to put his hand in his pocket for this, did you?)

I did what I had to. I brought it to him.

He didn't say a word. Hey, he was the captain!

We resumed patrol. In the afternoon, it was our turn. We got a coffee and went to the pier. It wasn't our sector—not a cardinal sin.

Another car pulled onto the pier. It was the two officers who had turned in the report on that gambler.

After a while Bob said, "Jim, there's the captain."

He walks to our car.

I got out, and he said to me, "I waited ten minutes for you to leave."

He wrote us up, and the other two, and charged us with a myriad of violations.

Pause for a minute.... Why him and not the sergeant on patrol? The pier was a good distance from the station house. Had he been following the other crew for bringing more attention to his command?

And why did he tell me he waited a while for us to leave?

I bring up these questions because I was involved as a sergeant in a gambling case, and I learned how the game was played.

Never the less, can't cry over spilled milk.

He played his hand with a too-hardened fist. They knocked our charges down. We lost our seat in the car and had to go to the trial room to plead to the charges. Quite formal.

My organization sent someone to represent me.

They pled my case, "Officer Cocalas is a veteran of the U.S. Navy. He is married and has two children and has three Excellent Police Citations."

Then it was Bob's turn. "Officer Mullany was a marine and saw action in the South Pacific—"

Bob interrupted, "—and I killed twelve Japs!"

The decision came down in a few days: Loss of two vacation days and back to foot patrol. And boy, did the sergeants have their knives sharpened.

Oh, by the way, this was the first complaint of three.

I ain't bragging.

LATE TOUR HIDE AND SEEK

Well, I was back on foot patrol. What's that old song they sang during the war? Oh yeah. "We did it before, and we could do it again." The only guys who weren't sorry were the two guys who replaced us.

I'd show up for work, change into my uniform, find out what post I had and go on patrol.

They switched Bob's squad, so we wouldn't be working together. The worst part was the physical part. Walking tires you out, and before long, I'd be looking for a place to sit and grab a smoke, playing cat and mouse with the sergeant.

During the day tours or the four-till-midnight, it wasn't too bad, but the late tour was a challenge. The sergeants on the late tours would spend half the tour riding and supervising and then take the switchboard. They were supposed to physically see each man on post, and to sign their memo books. (CYA)

Then they would change assignments.

In the late sixties and early seventies, we turned out at least ten men on foot. Two on West 42 between Seventh Avenue and Eighth Avenue, two on Eighth Avenue between West 27 and West 34, and a couple on West 34 between Fifth and Eighth.

I usually got the glass post on Broadway from West 34 north to West 38.

It became a game of wits. The sooner the sarge could sign the books, the sooner he could relax. I knew all the drivers, and they told me they purposely went to my post last, after signing everyone else's book.

I wouldn't dare leave my post. I'd have been a fool to.

I'd find a deep doorway, and when I figured he'd be around, I'd step in.

It was getting close to 3 a.m. The driver would put a plaque in the window to alert you that it was the supervisor's car. He would slowly cruise down Broadway. When he would pass me, I'd rap my nightstick on the ground, and the brake lights would go on. I'd walk to the curb and as they backed up, the window would roll down.

He'd say, "Where you been?"

"Here, sarge. You passed right by me."

I couldn't play that game too often. Some were mean, but not stupid.

I'd tell myself, *You better watch your butt, Cocalas. You're getting too old to go back to roofing.*

NINTH AVENUE TRIFECTA

The platoon had turned out, and I was walking to my post, when I heard, "Cocalas, wait up."

It was one of the toughest cops in the precinct and the most brutal and a drinker. With him was a carbon copy.

I slowed up, and we crossed Seventh Avenue going toward Eighth. I had Ninth Avenue from West 38 to West 42. They had Eighth Avenue. I walked with them up Eighth for a bit, until they stopped at the first bar.

We were doing a 4 p.m. to midnight, and they hadn't even gotten to their post yet.

I'm not a drinker, and I'm not a fool, so I said, "I'll see you guys later."

I continued up Eighth and cut over to Ninth. I passed the Terminal Bar. The place was quiet, but it was early.

I walked up to West 42 and peeked around the corner, checking out the area.

Not too bad, I thought, *but it's early.*

I started back toward West 39. There was an all-night fruit and vegetable stand there. The guy who had the night shift had been the subject of horseplay by some tough guys from a club on West 39.

One night, when I was still assigned a sector, I rode up on one of them, while he had the poor man in a headlock and was messing up his hair.

I got out of the car. He saw me and let go of the fruit man. I said, "Why don't you stop busting this guy's balls?"

"Mind your business," he told me.

He walked up to me in an aggressive manner, so I shoved him into some crates of fruit. My partner got out of the car in case things got out of hand.

They didn't.

This man's boss came out of the club and told him to knock it off.

Let me tell you about this guy, the one who'd been harassing the fruit seller. A few months later, he was sitting at a local bar where everybody knew everybody.

The owner, a woman from the neighborhood, was in the rear either counting receipts or doing other business stuff. It was about 9 or 10 p.m.

In walked two men, who were part of a westside gang. They headed for the rear, where the owner was. From where our guy was sitting on a stool at the bar, he could watch the whole scenario taking place in the back. They were robbing the owner.

As they were walking out, he confronted them, saying something like, "Why would you do that in this neighborhood?"

They hit him on the head with a bottle.

He disarmed one of them and began firing.

When we arrived, he was sitting on the stool with his hanky to his head. The two tough guys, who had tried to rob the bar, were lying on the floor. I remember one had been shot in the front of the head, but the bullet didn't exit. Instead the back of his head looked like it had a tennis ball wanting to come out!

And the fellow who'd taken care of that situation so effectively was the guy I'd pushed into the fruit crates.

Whew!

Now getting back to me walking my post on Ninth Avenue....

There was a funeral parlor off Ninth. I knew the owner. Sometimes, I'd sit with him and talk, when he didn't have anyone laid out.

One night, as I walked by, I noticed the lights were still on in the office.

I went inside, and he said, "Jim would you do me a favor? I have to bring a body downstairs."

"Huh? Uh, okay."

We went upstairs, where he had an elderly man dressed in a brown suit. (I made up my mind right then that, when I go to meet my Maker, I don't want to be wearing a brown suit.) What made it even more odd was that he was lying on a table, and he was so stiff that we could carry him without any center support. The mortician had the upper part, and I was at the feet.

We got him downstairs and into the coffin, and I left.

"Thanks," he yelled as I was walking out the door.

I asked myself, *Did I just carry a body from upstairs and put it in a coffin? Well, I'm glad the tour's almost over.* I wouldn't tell anyone about that...until now.

I signed out, changed and I was almost out the door, when I heard the desk officer say, "Cocalas, did you see So-and-So?" (The tough, brutal drinker I mentioned earlier.)

"Yeah," I said, "when we turned out."

"Take a ride up Eighth and see if you can find him."

There's no arguing with the desk officer.

I figured I'd give it a shot, and if I didn't see him on my first run up Eighth, I was going home.

There he was on Eighth and West 33.

I beeped the horn. He threw his nightstick at my car. He was reaching for his gun!

Another drunken bum.

I'm going home.

REMEMBER KITTY GENOVESE

Anybody know who Kitty Genovese was? She was murdered by a low life in Queens on March 13, 1964.

What makes this more heart-wrenching was that in the initial assault he stabbed her, not fatally, but was scared off by people who heard screams and yelled, "What's going on down there?"

That was probably the only thing that prevented Kitty from being killed...at that time.

She laid there, helpless, hurt, and calling for help. No one came, except the killer, who returned and stabbed her again and again.

Still no one came.

The investigation revealed that THIRTY-EIGHT people heard her call for help, and again no one came. The killer was caught, convicted and sentenced to death.

Appeals vacated the death sentence and gave him life

without parole.

Oh, yeah. He escaped and was captured again, but not before he broke into a house and raped a woman!

Is your heart hurting as is mine now?

I'm going to tell you of an incident similar to what happened to Kitty Genovese. Only someone heard and did something. Me.

I was assigned to Central Park for some detail or other. I remember it was drizzling, and I was dying for a smoke and to get out of the raincoat which wasn't exactly working.

I was so far from the event, I didn't know it was cancelled. No walkie talkie or cell phones in those days.

I was close to Central Park West. Across the street, on the corner, there was a small hotel. It wasn't even in the precinct I was assigned to. It was either the 20 Precinct or the 24.

I hopped across the street, entered the entrance to the lobby, and lit up.

I was exchanging hellos with the doorman when I heard a yell.

"Did you hear that?" I asked him.

He said, "Sounds like it came from up the block."

I stepped out and started walking up the street, lined with brownstone buildings and basement apartments.

I heard it again and started to jog, looking at the downstairs level of each building I passed.

At one apartment entrance, down a few steps, a man had a woman in a choke hold with one arm and in the other hand he had a knife!

"DROP THE KNIFE!" I yelled.

She broke away and ran into the apartment.

He was about four steps down. I had my gun pointed at him.

Sergeant Edward Johnson had been stabbed to death after the perp was shot at least six times, and I was going to shoot this guy?!

What I did next, I can't explain.

I cocked the gun.

He dropped the knife, and I could hear sirens. I took a step or two down the stairs toward him. He put his head down and tried to bully past me.

I gave him a good crack on the top of his head with my gun.

Then, the cops were all over us.

I heard some boss tell me, "Uncock your gun and holster it!"

I did.

Then he asked me, "What precinct you from?"

"Fourteen," I told him. "I was on a detail in the park, and I heard screams."

He said, "Great work. Come on. We'll give you a ride to the precinct."

I told him, "Boss, I don't want the collar."

"Why?"

"I can't get involved. I've got two young kids at home, and my wife's not up to par.

"Okay, officer," he said. "Good job."

After I signed out from the Central Park Precinct, I was going home and feeling pretty good about myself.

Giving that arrest away cost me a good commendation. I think about it every once in a while.

Then I think of Kitty Genovese, and I don't feel sorry for myself any more.

ANOTHER CHANCE IN RMP

I was still walking posts, being checked on by sergeants, get-ting strike posts, getting Broadway on midnights to watch the glass, and...the degrading, boring task of staying in front of a haberdasher, who had been burglarized a few times.

The store was on the corner of Fifth Avenue and West 33 across from the Empire State Building. The owner, or corpo-ration representing the store, must have had some influence with somebody high up to get that kind of protection. The store was covered from the time it closed until it opened the next morning.

If you had it on the late tour, you were stuck. No coffee break. You were supervised by the sergeant on patrol, the borough shoofly, and the duty captain. Each were obligated to sign your memo book.

The sector car would sometimes bring you coffee and

would take a risk by letting you sit in their car to smoke.

Just by chance, (You don't believe that, do you?) if you shook the doors hard enough, it would set off a silent alarm in the Holmes Security office. I think the office was only a couple of blocks away. It wouldn't be more than ten minutes before the Holmes people showed up.

"What's up, fellas?" they'd ask. "You been here the whole time?"

"Yeah."

They'd open the door, reset the alarm, do a fast look around, and leave.

Anything to pass the time.

I was preparing to do an 8 to 4 tour, and the lieutenant behind the desk called out, "Cocalas, the captain wants to see you. He's in his office."

We had a new captain, Captain James P. O'Brian.

I wasn't worried, but I was curious. The last time I'd been called to the captain's office I'd gotten him a coffee, a danish, the *New York Times*, charges, and two vacation days deducted.

Well here goes, I thought as I entered and saluted.

"Patrolman Cocalas," he said, "I hear you got a raw deal. So, I'm putting you back in a sector. You know Merryman? He's your partner."

"Thank you, sir. I won't let you down."

Wow! I knew Larry. A tall, nice looking guy, married with a couple of kids.

We hit it off.

While sharing a meal he'd read the *Times* while I read the *Daily News*. He didn't smoke but never made an issue about me smoking. He'd just open the window, I'd get the message and ditch the cigarette. Our wives met and they seem to get along.

His height was an asset.

On one occasion, we were called to a bar about a disorderly drunk they wanted removed. I walked in first, and the drunk laughed and said, "*You're* going to throw me out?"

"No," I told him. "Not me. Him."

Larry had just walked in. The guy looked at him, said, "No problem," and left.

Another time, we arrested a robbery suspect. It was easy because of the description given. He was wearing a tuxedo with sneakers. There's a photo of Larry and the dope wearing the tuxedo.

On another occasion, we were at the scene of a fire, and we were carrying a stretcher with an injured fireman on it.

My back went out, but I wouldn't dare drop the guy. I made it back to the car. There was no way I'd go sick. (I had also hurt it putting in a regulator for my cousin, who would later become a detective in narcotics.)

It'll be okay, I thought, *if I can rest a little*.

Not that night.

We got a job in a hallway—a disorderly man. We entered, and he became belligerent.

We figured we could talk him out of anything that was bothering him. No dice.

Larry said, "Okay, time to go," and we grabbed him.

Whoa, my back was killing me!

I let go of him and sat on the steps. Larry was still holding him. When the guy saw me, he said to Larry, "I'll go!" And he told me, "I'm sorry."

I said, "Larry can you finish the tour?"

"Yeah."

When I got home I took a muscle relaxer. Darvon, I think.

I lay down flat, grabbed the furniture, and Bobbie pulled my legs. I put a brace under me, and I listened to some soft music, giving the relaxer a chance to work. In about a half an hour, I was good to go.

FIRST RIOT

One thing about police work—whether you're walking a post, assigned a radio car, or working inside doing clerical work—is that you have no control on what may be coming.

That's exactly what happened in the city one day, and it called for the mobilization of most of the police units.

There had been an incident of a shooting by a police officer. An off-duty lieutenant fatally shot a young black student. The reason, location, names, dates, accusations, investigations can be found on Wikipedia.

If I remember correctly, as a result, the rules within the department were changed regarding the use of deadly force, while pursuing an individual you believed had committed a felony.

All this occurred in the summer of 1964.

I was doing a 4 p.m. to midnight tour, but after we were in

the muster room, they told us we were going up to Harlem. The talk—in the navy we called it "scuttle butt"—was about a cop shooting a black.

All I knew was that the "broom" (an older cop past retirement age and assigned light duty around the station) came up from the storage room with WW2 air raid warden helmets!

Gulp!

Hey, this looks serious, I told myself.

Let me explain how I felt at the time....

In the navy, I'd survived for three days on bread and water. I'd been in fist fights, entered bar rooms in the middle of a donnybrook (a free-for-all brawl), been to fires, made gun arrests, and had always done what was expected of me. But when they brought up those helmets, I knew I was about to experience something new, and I wasn't happy about it.

They piled us into a bus, and we rode uptown to Mount Morris Park. There were hundreds of us from precincts all over the city. They gave us our locations and turned us out.

The guys from the 14 Precinct were assigned West 125 and Seventh Avenue. I was in good company with Tommy Stuart, a WWII veteran; Artie Hensel, Korean combat veteran; and me, a Korean war veteran, who'd pushed planes while his ship was in the Mediterranean Sea. And then there was Danny Fortuna, who was a legend.

It wasn't exactly a war zone. Our orders were to hold the corners and not allow anyone onto West 125. It seemed like the epicenter of the riot. The crowd was breaking windows, looting, setting fires and not allowing any traffic to enter the street.

At that point, they were concentrated in the middle of the block. Somebody had decided to confine the riot to that one area. Whoever thought of that tactic hadn't considered allowing the mob to disperse onto either avenue, thereby thinning the crowd.

Around the corner came about four cars filled with Tactical Control Force (TPF) personnel. One of the requirements of being in that command was that you had to be over six feet tall. These big guys spilled out of the cars and were making use of their night sticks.

The crowd started running in all directions. A lot of them were coming right at us.

I remember a young guy in a white tee-shirt, covering his head with his arms, tucking his head down to his chest, and running right between me and Danny.

We both swung right and left at the mass of people charging us. I got hit in my knee with one of my fellow cop's missed swings. Excruciating pain! I landed on my butt, right in front of the Hotel Theresa.

In spite of all the pain, a thought came to me. *I'm hurt! I'll be getting out of here!* But when I looked up, there were no police officers in sight. They were chasing people down Seventh Avenue.

What I did see was a crowd of angry people. I heard them cursing me, insulting me, the color of my skin, and my heritage. More importantly, they were screaming about how they were going to end my life! (Hey fellas, would you accept an apology?)

I got up, leaned against the building, and pulled my gun. That stopped them...momentarily.

Through the crowd, I saw my sergeant. I called out to him.

He charged into the group, and they fled. He waved an RMP down, and they took me into the 28 station house.

Inside was chaos. Everywhere there were hurt officers, prisoners cuffed and sitting on the floor, ambulance attendants treating people. I found a place to sit. No one was paying attention to me.

My pain eased. I was starting to relax.

"Yo, Cocalas. How ya' doing? You all right?" It was Tommy.

"Yeah, I'm all right. I got hit in the knee."

"How is it now?"

"Okay, I guess."

"Come on then. All the guys are waiting for you."

"I've gotta fill out an aided card."

He knew I was stalling. "You could do that later. Come on."

I knew I couldn't con him or the other guys.

I went back in the street.

WELCOME TO THE 23 PRECINCT

G etting back to the precinct after the riots....

I realized what Detective Johnny Meyers meant when I told him I was assigned the 14 Precinct as my first command. After spending time up in Harlem during the riot, it slowly came to me that I knew so little of the city, its neighborhoods, the racial makeup of its residents, prejudices on both sides. How naive could I have been?

When I was in the navy, I slept on a canvas rack, inches from a black sailor from Detroit. His name was Stewart. One day, we were going into Portsmouth together. He said he was going to the movie there.

We sat in the rear of the bus together, and when the bus reached a certain part of the town, he stood up.

I told him, "This isn't the stop."

He said, "It is for me."

It didn't dawn on me what was going on, until the bus driver explained to me, "They wouldn't let him in the movie where you're going."

I've already told you about the black sailor named Reginald Benedict Lewis, who brought me orange juice, when I was serving three days with just bread and water. He prevented me from hitting a racist petty officer with a wrench after the guy sucker punched me. Reginald saved me from serving a term in Leavenworth.

I remember the white/black water fountains, the white/black bathrooms. That was in 1952.
We haven't progressed too far, have we?

Back on patrol, Larry told me he was going to study for the next sergeants' test.
I remember talking to a detective from the 14 Squad who was going to be promoted to sergeant.
"Why would you do that?" I asked him. "You're in one of the best squads in the city."
He gave me an economics lesson: "From sergeant, the next test will be the lieutenants', then the captains'. All civil service appointments are by your scores on a test. After that, promotion to deputy inspector, full inspector, and up the ladder is granted by merit or by the proverbial rabbi."
Well, I hung onto Larry's coat tails We studied at his home, in the radio car, and at schools run by retired bosses.
He scored way high on the list and was one of the first to be called. He was assigned the 24 Precinct. But there was no stopping him. He took the lieutenant's test, same results. The captain's test, same results. It took him only a few years.
Later, I learned he'd made deputy inspector and was the commanding officer of the 105 Precinct.
While he was climbing that ladder, I got promoted to sergeant in June 1969. Guess what? No fanfare from anybody in

the station. I showed up there with my new sergeant's shield on my chest, went to my locker to retrieve some things, and when I came down, I swear, neither the lieutenant nor the sergeant looked up.

And I worked there 12 years.

My new command was the 23 Precinct. It runs from East 86 north to East 106 and from Fifth Avenue east to the East River. The station house was on East 104 between Third Avenue and Lexington Avenue.

I was to report the next day, a Saturday, for a midnight to 8 a.m.

I took the 59th Street Bridge to Third Avenue and headed north. When I got to East 86, I thought, *Hey, this ain't so bad.*

I kept driving north.

When I got to 96 Street, it changed drastically. Compared to 86 Street, it looked like a slum.

Over the years, Harlem has become somewhat "gentrified," a change that hasn't been welcomed by all. With higher property prices, a lot of poor people can no longer afford to remain in their homes.

But back in the 1980s there was a crack epidemic, not to mention extreme poverty, and it was a dangerous, difficult place to live, raise a family—and work. Especially if you were a cop.

As I drove past 104, I peeked up the street. Were they having a riot in the block?

I stopped in front of the station house and was getting out when somebody said, "You can't park there."

I told him, "I'm Sergeant Cocalas. Just got assigned here."

"Okay, Sarge. I'll keep an eye it."

"What's going on in the block?"

"Just a normal Saturday night."

I went inside, introduced myself to the desk officer. I got assigned a locker upstairs, changed, came down and turned out the men.

My driver was a young officer. We started on patrol, and he said, "Where to?"

"Just make the rounds of the avenues first."

He started down Second Avenue.

At about 102 Street he said, "Look, Sarge. They're welcoming you to the precinct.

I looked over, and there was a woman defecating between two cars.

SELF-MUTILATION

I was getting the feel of the precinct, and the troops were getting to feel me out, too.

Is he a pushover?

They found out soon enough.

During a day tour, there was a call of a "1013, assist patrolman at East 85th Street off of Second Avenue, units responding?"

"23 sergeant responding. Sector boy responding. Sector Charlie responding."

"Sector Adam, no further assistance required."

"Sector Adam, what's the condition?"

My driver and I had arrived, when I heard this, and I didn't see sector Adam on the scene.

He was just coming around the corner. The original call had been unnecessary. It was a dispute between a sanitation officer and a building superintendent.

I radioed, "23 sergeant to Central. No further assistance needed. Unnecessary call."

"1004. All units resume patrol."

I wave down sector Adam and asked them, "Why did you call off the 1013, when you weren't even on the scene?"

They said, "We figured there was enough cars here."

"Go to the precinct. I'll meet you there."

I went to the precinct. There was a lieutenant behind the desk. I explained what happened.

He said, "I know the guy. He's been in that sector so long he thinks he's immune."

I told him, "I want to take him out of the car for a couple of tours. I'll tell the roll call. 'Look, I'd like him out of the car, starting this tour.'"

"You got it, Sarge."

The operator of sector Adam came into the house and I said to him, "You got the station house post for the rest of the tour."

He was stunned.

I told his partner, "Pick up somebody on post, and he'll ride with you for the rest of the tour."

Guys are like a bunch of washerwomen when it comes to gossip.

I found out from my driver that not many guys liked him. Their reasoning was: He had the most lucrative sector for a good meal for nothing but the cost of a tip for the waiter.

Hey, that's just the way it was.

At that point, I was tiptoeing. There were other sergeants working in that precinct. I didn't want to be ostracized by the rest of the bosses.

But the truth was, I had more time in than most of them. They knew I was intent on doing the job my way.

The 23 Precinct really was two precincts sharing the same area. From East 86 Street to East 96 was the more desirable area to live in, shop in, dine in, and to patrol. The upper half not so.

A sector car requested the sergeant's car to meet him at an

address on East 96. When I got there, I was met by an officer standing outside. He was pale.

"What's up?" I asked him.

"You gotta see this, Sarge. The first-floor apartment."

I followed him inside and there, lying on a piece of plastic, was a dead, nude, white, male in a fetal position.

There was blood on the plastic.

There wasn't much anyone could do but wait for the detectives to show up.

The ambulance arrived, and they also had to wait.

The detectives arrived and asked the ambulance people to turn the body over so they could determine where the blood had come from.

They did.

Someone had removed his penis and testicles. They were under him, along with a knife.

I secured the scene, the detectives and the attendants proceeded with their duties, and I resumed patrol.

Later, the detectives interviewed his wife, and it was determined he had inflicted the wounds himself!

That's how they did it on East 96 Street.

Below 96 Street, it was done differently.

I received a call to meet a sector car on Fifth Ave and East 87. The sector car was waiting, as was an attorney for the family who lived in the apartment we were about to enter. The attorney had been called by the occupant's relatives.

There in the bathroom was a young woman in a blue negligee, draped over the bowl. Dead—no doubt.

We found a suicide note.

She had been preparing to do that for some time. She had a dog and had made arrangements to put him in a kennel.

This is my assumption and no one else's: I believe she took an overdose of sleeping pills and was lying in bed, waiting to meet her Maker. She got the urge to throw up and rushed to the bathroom, where she died.

God forgive me for thinking at that time, *Lady, if you could have seen what you'd look like now, you never would have done this.*

TIME TO MOVE

It was a quiet, late tour. I thought, *Another hour and it'll be over*. I'd be on my way home to see how well my wife fared with our two teenagers, without me.

I hadn't heard any gripes from my son, but a few days before, my daughter had been in a confrontation with another girl. From what my daughter had told me, it sounded more threatening, more serious, than the usual kid squabbles.

I'd gone to the school and sat in the cafeteria and watched. Sure enough, she was approached by a rough-looking girl, whom I assumed was the one she was having a problem with.

Before I intervened, a teacher got up and said something, and the girl went back to her seat.

Time to move.

Over time, our neighborhood had grown steadily worse, tougher, meaner. I saw evidence of it every day on the streets, in the local businesses, in my neighbors' homes. And now it had seeped into the schools.

I was concerned for my family's safety. And there was no way that I could leave for work with that kind of worry on my back.

I spoke to my wife. She was disappointed but understood.

We had worked hard to make that house one of the best on the block. We were the first to paint over stucco that had never been painted before. It was a chore. I'd dip a brush in the paint, put the brush to the stucco and swoosh! It would suck it right up.

I went to the paint store, and the clerk asked if I had brushed the stucco first with a wire brush.

Huh?

I tried that, and sure enough, it worked. Painting it became a family affair. My sister came over to help out. My wife was pregnant but not too far along. The O'Leary's and Joan and Lou Ruiz helped.

But I had to put all that on the back burner. Being a police officer and having anything else on your mind is not a healthy thing.

So, there we were, my driver and I, sitting in the radio car overlooking the East River, and he spotted someone in the water about 100 feet out. The tide was swiftly taking him north. We notified Central, and as he passed a fireboat anchorage, they were able to bring him aboard.

The sector in that area called for the supervisor to meet them. That was me.

When we got there, the guy explained he'd been sitting too near the edge and had slipped in.

When we asked if he'd "slipped in" intentionally, he got indignant. "No! Of course, I wasn't going to commit suicide! My jacket's still there where I was sitting!"

I told the sector car to take him back to where he'd been. I thanked the fireboat people. And we went back to where we were parked.

We had a little talk.

"Shall we get coffee?"

"Nah, the tour's almost over."

Or so we thought.

We glanced over at the river, and here came that bobbing head, going right past us.

No need to call the fireboat.

They grabbed him again.

This time, I ordered the sector car crew to take him to Bellevue, (a psychiatric hospital, for you non-New Yorkers).

Let's get out of here!

The next few days off, I decided to forego golf and Bobbie and I looked at some houses in a town that I had a hard time pronouncing.

We didn't sign with anyone, so we just drove around. It was a beautiful fall day. I kept thinking to myself, *What a day for golf!*

We drove down this tree-lined street with some nice homes. I was driving slowly, enjoying the ride, when I spotted a garage in the rear of a home. It looked like a Dutch barn. I drove around the block to show it to Bobbie. It was situated at the end of a gravel driveway. I had thoughts of a workshop, etc.

Snap out of Jimmy, I said to myself. *It's probably out of your range.*

We went to a realtor on my next day off. I thought, *There goes another day I won't be playing golf.*

We met the realtor, and he showed us some nice homes. I was ready to sign on a few of them, but Bobbie said, "Let's look at some more."

The realtor took us down a street that I remembered from

the week before. He pulled up diagonally across from the house with the Dutch barn-like garage. He was talking about how he was having a tough time negotiating with the owner.

I wasn't listening.

I told the realtor, "If you can get the price close to what I can afford, I'll buy it!"

He blurted out, "You didn't even see the inside."

My wife didn't say a word. We went back to his office, and he contacted the owner.

That was in November.

We moved in early February.

COPS MISBEHAVING

East 86 Street on a Saturday night was a Mecca for enter-tainment. The Lorelei served great German food. The Corso was the place to go for Latin music and dancing. And the Papaya King had all sorts of soft drinks. It opened on East 86 and Third Avenue in 1932, the year I was born. (I just looked it up on the computer and it's still there!) There was rarely any trouble on that block.

Actually, Yorkville was an upscale neighborhood, unless you went past 96 Street.

We were called to a new bar-type restaurant called the Arabian Nights. When we arrived, there were two detectives talking to the owner, who was standing behind the bar. We sat in stools in front of the bar.

He was lamenting that he'd received veiled threats about opening. I surmised that somebody was trying to get their sticky fingers into his business.

As we were talking, a male came in, walked past us, and continued to a downstairs bathroom. Suddenly, the owner seemed hesitant about talking. I figured he recognized the gent who had gone down to the bathroom. In a few minutes, the guy came back up and walked out the door.

The owner whispered to us, "That was one of the guys who's been threatening me."

The detectives were about to say something, when we saw smoke coming from the basement. I think the owner was having second thoughts about opening.

I never found out the final outcome. I was transferred before the investigation was over.

On one of those warm summer nights, many people were congregated in front of the Lorelei, mostly young and some drunk. As we were cruising by, we were waved down by one of the officers assigned to that sector. His partner was talking to some young people, and I could see it wasn't going well.

The officer saw me, walked over to us, and quietly told me that the man he was having the not-too-friendly chat with was a cop.

I walked over to guy. The young lady he was with was tugging on his sleeve.

I asked him, "Are you a police officer?"

"Yes, Sarge."

"Let me see your shield." All his bravado melted away. "And your service revolver."

He meekly complied. I took both from him.

I walked back to the car, got in, and told my driver to take me to the station. As we were pulling away, I gave a last look back. The kid was crying.

When I got back to the house, I told the sergeant on the desk what happened and to keep the shield and the gun in the drawer. I also told him he could expect a humbled young man to come in and pick them up.

I spoke to the sergeant later, and he said the kid came back sober with his girlfriend, thanked him, and said to tell the other sarge that he'd learned a lesson. I hope he did.

That was an easy one. This next one was scary.

I was called to the house and the lieutenant gave me an address on Park Avenue. Not the Park Avenue above East 96 Street, but the Park Avenue close to East 86.

Seemed there was a psychiatrist treating a police officer from our department. The officer had an appointment soon and had requested that a superior officer be present while he discussed his problems.

Let me tell you, that didn't sound kosher. I'm sure there was nothing in the police bible, the rules and procedures, to cover that.

When we showed up, the doctor told us that he was afraid of his patient. As he was speaking, the officer was standing in the doorway. He was a huge fellow with a shoulder holster and a non-regulation revolver sticking out of it.

The doctor vanished.

I started talking to the officer. Charlie, my driver, was positioning himself on the opposite side of the cop. (Thank God for Charlie.) The officer stepped back, and we moved forward.

I was explaining to him why we were there, and when we got close enough, I snatched the gun out of his holster.

He stood there dumbfounded. I told him to pick it up at the station house, and we left.

The doctor was still nowhere to be seen.

PSYCHO WITH A BUTCHER KNIFE

On any summer's night in the 23 Precinct, mostly above East 96, the streets would be crowded with people, looking to have a good time.

Occasionally, some would light a match to the emotions of the crowd, and all hell would break loose. And if the police were involved, it could turn into an inferno.

On one such occasion, the fire started.

At Lexington Avenue and East 104, a crowd had gathered in the middle of the intersection. A man stood, brandishing a knife. Not just a knife, but a butcher's knife *and* a meat cleaver.

It seemed everyone in the area knew this guy. No doubt someone had called the police.

When one car arrived, and then the second car, and then I showed up, they became even more agitated.

I heard shouts of, "Leave him alone!" and Spanish curses

that I'd heard before.

"He's sick, man!" somebody yelled.

"He ain't hurting nobody!"

None of the cops would go near him. If he moved toward anyone, the crowd would back away.

If he moved toward any of the cops, they would back away.

A standoff.

The longer we stayed, the larger the crowd grew and the more the macho men in the crowd taunted us.

What happened was like an awkward ballet.

One of the cops got into a sector car and clipped him, just enough to knock him off balance. Another used his night stick, hoping to score a hit on the guy's skull and get him to drop the knife and cleaver. But at the last second, the man turned his head in such a way that he caught it, full on, and the intended base hit looked more like a home run!

He wobbled. Swayed. The crowd roared. We thought he'd drop the weapons for sure, maybe even go down.

But no!

Still holding on to the meat cleaver and knife he staggered toward me.

I took out my gun, and the crowd started to scream!

I was retreating, but he was still coming toward me.

I remember thinking, *I'll be damned if anybody thinks I'm going to get stabbed to death on the streets of Spanish Harlem!*

Whack!

Charlie got his home run. The man was down.

I called to the team who had the sector and told them, "Get him in the car and take him to Metropolitan Hospital. You guys, back in the cars. Don't worry about the crowd."

Sometimes, that's how you had to handle things above 96 Street.

A WELL-PRESERVED FURRIER

While wracking my brain to write some of my experiences during my time at the 23 Precinct, I neglected to mention my beloved brother, Anthony. He was a window trimmer, who worked out of a haberdasher on East 86. On one of my walking tours in the precinct to acclimate myself to the area, I spotted him, and he was as surprised as I was.

Anthony, who passed too early, was six years younger than I was. He had an artistic talent, as did my father. I remember visiting him at Fort Dix in New Jersey, when he was in that six-month active duty deal and owed the army a few years in the reserves.

I used to kid him about that.

Rest in Peace, Brother.

Now to the more gruesome part of being a police officer. No not the part where you're giving parking tickets, but the part where you're ordered to search a long dead human being.

There was a call by neighbors in a four-story apartment building, complaining of a dog barking and a smell in a hallway. Uh-oh.

I knew what that was going to be, only it turned out to be more bizarre than you can imagine.

When we pulled up to the address, one of the officers was standing by his sector car.

"What's up?" I asked him. "Where's your partner?"

"Upstairs, Sarge. Second floor. We got a DOA. We're waiting for the squad."

"That bad, eh?"

I left him there with my driver.

There is no describing the stench. Unless you've smelled it before, you can't imagine.

I could hear the yapping dog.

The door to the apartment was open, and as I got closer, I found the reason. There was a decaying body blocking the door from being opened fully.

Gingerly, I stepped over the body and entered a combination kitchen, small living room, and bedroom.

Seated in the kitchen was the other officer, talking softly to a middle-aged woman, sitting opposite him.

I didn't interfere. I looked at the body, a male white who had been dead more than a few days. It was face up, and the features looked almost mummified.

Later, I spoke to the detectives and found out the man was a furrier from Midtown, and he would occasionally show up here for a sexual encounter. In fact, there had been posters issued by Missing Persons, meaning he had been missing more than a few days.

He and the woman had been in bed together, and he must have had a heart attack. She had panicked, then managed to dress him and get him off the bed.

She tried to get him out of the apartment.

When she realized she couldn't move him any farther, she left him where he was, and she went to work. Hence the dog barking.

When she returned, the poor woman cleaned up the fluids seeping from the body.

We called emergency service for gas masks, and I ordered the officer, who had been by the car when I'd first arrived, to search him.

He pleaded with me not to make him do it. He was getting sick.

I relented, and his partner did it.

The body had to be removed. The dog was sent to the pound. Missing Persons was notified. And the women had to be evaluated by a doctor.

You think we earned our pay that day?

NEW ASSIGNMENT

The police department was in chaos during the late 1960s and the early 70s. Beside the demonstrations against the Vietnam War, there were investigations of police corruption, culminating with arrests in Brooklyn and the conviction of William Phillips, a former plainclothesman, for murder.

The brains at the top decided that the designation of "plainclothesman" was tainted, so they came up with a new one. If you had been in the former division office in the borough, you were now in OCCB. The Office of the Criminal Control Bureau.

Oh yeah. Call the same thing by a different name and that'll fix it. Wrong.

They also decided that the objective of the OCCB would be to concentrate on the criminals at the top, and pretty much ignore the middle men and the guys on the bottom.

The street smart, run-of-the mill crooks, like lower level drug dealers and policy operators, (I'll explain who they are later) soon realized they could work and not worry about being summarily arrested. If they were observed breaking the law on their post, it would only result in a report being submitted. That report would be stuck in a folder with other reports, and a case would be built with the hopes, rather dreams, of getting the head of that particular operation.

While all this case building was going on, the lower level people operated without fear.

On occasion, that resulted in police officers making phony calls to locations where the violations (like bags of marijuana, policy slips, etc.) were obvious, and later, they would testify that the violations had been in plain sight.

All in all, just going for the top guys might have been a good idea, but it was easier said than done.

I was still assigned to the 23 Precinct as a patrol supervisor. There was a move to put older, more experienced, supervisors in OCCB. I was chosen.

Before I left, I said goodbye to a couple of the men I'd worked with—Sergeants Joe Mannino and Ray Kelly, who rose up the ranks and eventually became the Police Commissioner. You heard the expression the cream comes to the top? Well, that was certainly the case with Ray.

Leaving those guys behind was the bad part; the rest promised to be all good. Like when I got home and got to tell my wife of my new assignment and the steady tours I would be working. Her topsy-turvy world would be less chaotic, and she could plan things based on a schedule that wouldn't change every five days.

I was sent to the Police Academy off Third Avenue for training on how the policy game was played and the hierarchy of the criminals involved.

Here's what I learned....

First, you have the actual writer of the bets. They usually

operate out of local businesses like barber shops, bars, and candy stores and such. Then there's a runner who picks up the bets from those establishments. They pass it over to another guy who's a rung higher up the ladder, and eventually, he takes it to the bank. Not your local Chase or Bank of America, mind you. The "bank" is guy at the top. Getting him, the bank, was the objective.

Before I left the course, I found I was having trouble with my left eye. There was an eye clinic close by and, luckily, I was seen by the training doctor and not by the students.

He asked me, "Do you have a stressful job?"

"I'm a police officer," I told him.

"Do you ever get a tightening in your chest, when you're going on a job?"

"Yes."

"Well," he said, "you have a broken blood vessel in the vortex of your eye. There are two things we can do. One is: Give you a shot of cortisone in the eye. Or you can rest it for about six months, and it'll heal."

Guess which way I went.

Later, I told my wife, "Don't worry. The doctor says just not to be involved in anything stressful."

The very next day, I came home and saw my wife putting up wallpaper.

"Yikes! Bobbie," I told her. "The doctor said no stress!"

"That's why I'm doing it," she said. "So you don't have to."

How could you not love that girl?!

Finally, training was over, and I was assigned to the 13th Division. Several members of that division had been arrested when one of them had worn a wire, then testified against his fellow officers. So, needless to say, morale was low around there and tension was high.

I, on the other hand, was feeling pretty good about myself.

Picture this scenario: Anticipating the higher pay this new

assignment would bring, I had just sold my home to buy a
nicer one. And for the first time in my life, I was able to buy
a new F85 Oldsmobile. Since I was going to a new command
I was spruced up. New shirt and tie—all ready for my new
command.

As I walked into the office, I spotted an officer from the 23
Precinct.

"Hey, Jerry. How you doing?" With a big grin, I added, "I
got the bag! Am I too late?" (By "bag," I meant the imaginary
bag filled with bribe money.)

Oops.

The inspector, the commanding officer of the unit, called
out to me, "Sergeant. In my office."

His office was a glass cubicle.

"Do you know what happened here?" he asked.

"Sure, I do." How could I not have known? It was in all the
papers. A very big deal.

"Well, it's not anything to be joking about," he told me.

"Inspector," I said, "I know Jerry from the 23 Precinct. I
didn't mean anything by it."

He wasn't impressed with my defense. "Well, you'll be the
clerical sergeant—make sure the log's up to date."

Clerical sergeant?!

I'd been at my new assignment for less than five minutes
and they were already sticking me behind a desk?

No.

That wouldn't do.

"Inspector," I said, "I'm putting in for a transfer back to
patrol in the 23 Precinct. Or any patrol precinct."

He was stunned.

He realized how this would look "downtown." A new
supervisor wants a transfer after *one day* in his command!

Talk about drawing attention to yourself, when "attention"
was the last thing you needed.

At the end of the tour, he called me in his office. He made

no mention of our previous conversation.

He told me, "Go out with a unit tomorrow. Get the feel on how the units work."

Whew.

What a beginning!

WIRE TAPS AND LEAKS

At the OCCB of Brooklyn North, I was getting acquainted with the team I was to supervise. Some were on the ball, and a couple were real duds. I thought, maybe, when they were selected by their commanding officers to be transferred to OCCB, the bosses might have just wanted to dump a couple of unproductive officers from their commands. (I wonder if that's why I wound up there. You think?)

Sometimes, the teams worked together on a joint investigation, but most times we were competing with each other. In my unit I was fortunate to have an experienced, streetwise officer named Harry, who happened to live a few blocks from my parents' home in Flatbush.

On our first follow up of information received from uniformed officers, Harry and I were sitting in an unmarked car, watching for a particular vehicle to show up at a candy store.

We had its plate, make, and color.

"There it is!" I told him when the car drove up and stopped near the shop.

A guy got out, went into the store, and returned in minutes.

We followed him to about five locations, noting each address and the times he left. These bits of information would be important later, if we tried to obtain an arrest warrant from a judge. If we were lucky, maybe even an eavesdropping warrant.

Eventually, he led us to a corner in a residential area. He pulled over, parked, left his vehicle, and walked to another car. He gave the driver what looked like a paper sack.

That was when it got interesting and, between you and me, fun.

Let me tell you why, the way my street-smart driver explained it to me....

The bag was a valuable piece of evidence that we'd need for a judge, but, even better, we knew we were getting higher up the ladder of their organization. Harry said it was easy to tell, because of one little hierarchy behavior of theirs: The guy who got out of his car was lower in the system than the one who stayed in his and accepted the bag.

We were one step closer to what they called the "bank," the guy at the top!

We followed the man, who had received the bag, to another location. We watched as several other cars arrived. The drivers would walk over to his vehicle, drop off paper bags, and leave.

Again, we noted the plates, description, times, location.

Finally, my mentor said, "That's enough for today. Let's go back to the office and put this down on paper."

We could pick them up the next day and follow them a bit farther down the road and up the chain. There was no threat of ever losing them, because it would always be necessary for someone to pick up the "work" as it was called. All we had to do was to sit at one of the "drops" and wait for a car to show and pick up the work. He'd take us to the same location where we left them the day before. Simple.

It got tougher as you drew closer to the "bank." Smarter, more cautious, more trusted people, were involved. (We'll get back to this story later....)

Another member of my team was following an allegation of a bartender taking "action" (policy and bets) over the phone in a location that we thought was dealing in stolen goods.

He sat at the bar, watched the sports on TV, and became familiar with the owners and the different bartenders. Eventually, he started to make bets. He observed patrons making policy bets with the bartender, and at a certain time someone would come by and pick up the work. (The slips had to be collected before an exact time, to insure there'd be no action after the number was already out.)

We decided that our undercover had enough for him to explain to a judge why we needed an eavesdropping warrant in order to continue the investigation.

The judge agreed and gave us one.

In time, several more were issued as the investigations led to other crimes, which resulted in the suspension of a police officer and the murder of an informant we were supposed to be protecting!

Who could have foreseen what came next? Not me.

With all these chestnuts in the fire—145 people arrested on myriad charges and an investigation into the unidentified person who spoke to my mother about the murder on North 6th Street in 1936—here I was, waiting to be promoted to lieutenant. Instead, I was relieved of my command and sent back to uniform to the 67 Precinct. (I'll tell you later how all that came about.)

Back to Harry and me and our investigation....

At the office, we typed up and filed our observations on

the passing of policy slips.

Then, the next day, we returned to the place where we'd seen what we hoped was the last drop before they headed for the bank.

Wrong.

The guy drove to the parking lot of a department store and got out. He walked to a car and handed over a paper bag about the size of a half-gallon of milk.

He left.

The man with the bag waited for a few minutes, then took off.

Harry started to follow him. Slowly. Fortunately, the guy's car had distinctive brake lights.

He drove onto Queens Boulevard, and we stayed way back. Without any turn signal he made a U turn.

Anticipating what I was going to say, Harry told me, "I see him." (I told you he was good.)

The man in the car repeated the move—no signal and another U turn.

I didn't say anything, but I thought, *This guy's good, but we're better.*

We followed him to Bell Boulevard, where he parked, got out, and entered an apartment house.

It was time to back off. I knew the procedure—go to the office, type and file our observations.

The next day, we returned to the apartment on Bell Boulevard.

Our guy didn't show.

We backtracked.

We didn't see any of the cars that were previously involved in the transfer of the paper bag, just the ones picking up the work from stores, etc.

I asked Harry, "What happened?"

Without hesitation, he said, "Someone at the office is reading our summaries."

WHAT!?

SMALL DENT IN ORGANIZED CRIME

Okay, where were we? Oh yeah. Back at the bar with our undercover.

We applied for a warrant on the bar phone, got it. Nowadays, there's a procedure that prohibits the police—the ones who do all the investigating—from knowing how a location is set up or how it's coordinated with the phone company. But not so then.

We were told the location where this particular recorder would be. A member of the police's special unit was there and gave us a fast run down on pen recorders, like how to stop recording if the information wasn't pertinent to the case or was just mundane conversation. We thanked him and he left.

In a very few minutes, we heard our first incoming call. Here are the exact words of that short conversation: (Man's voice) "Larry's bar." (Woman's voice) "Listen, I work for the phone company. They're tapping your phone."

She hung up.

We were speechless and dumbfounded! We knew two things. All our work was for naught, and there was a leak somewhere.

The phone rang again, "Larry's bar. Yeah, Mike. They're playing tonight. Patriots are favored by nine. Okay, Mike, you got it. Patriots 20 times."

Wow, what just happened? The guy had just been warned, and he was still taking action? I had to speak to our officer sitting in the bar.

We drove by the bar and waited until the undercover got in his car and drove to the designated meeting place. We met him, and he told us what happened after the bartender got that call. He'd laughed it off, and said, "Some nut job from the phone company called and told me the phones are tapped." Then he went ahead and kept doing what he always did.

But there was a new wrinkle to this.

The undercover also told us that there was an off-duty police officer, who was out on medical leave, drinking at the bar. The guy got a call from his wife. She'd told him that the medical section had called their house and asked where he was. He told the bartender, "I gotta go. The PD's busting my chops, wants me to call in as soon as I get back home." We were forced to notify internal affairs. No one was happy about turning him in, but nobody would stick their neck out to save him. Neither would I.

Unfortunately, that officer dug himself an even bigger hole by giving the bartender a heads up when we tried to put another officer in there. He told the bartender straight up, "That new guy sitting over there is a cop."

None of us were sad when he was subpoenaed and became part and parcel of the 145 people we arrested. One of the charges was perjury.

Meanwhile, the policy investigation wasn't forgotten. Harry and I felt, with the leaks and our own working against us, getting the bank was going to be much tougher.

So, we tried a different tactic. We got arrest warrants based on our previous observations for any of the cars involved. Then we sat on the car who made the next to last delivery to the bank.

He was parked on a dead-end street. The guys who were dropping off to him could drive in easy enough, but they'd have to make a U-turn to get out.

After the first one pulled in and dropped off the work, he made a U-turn, and came out. We were waiting for him. As soon as he was out of the first guy's sight, we detained him, confiscated his car, and waited for the next one. We nabbed a total of five drivers and their cars.

I heard the Desk Officer where we were vouchering the cars wasn't happy about us creating all that extra work for him. But, in the end, we took out the runners and their cars and caused the operators of this organization to have to get new people from the neighborhood to pick up the work.

They did, and we did.

Every time a new face showed up at one of the locations, taking action and picking up "work," we arrested him and vouchered his car.

They were running out of people and decided to give a "zip" a chance. That's the term for new immigrant, looking to prove himself.

The "zip" was good, reckless. We were better. He made his rounds, and we decided to pull him over. He took off and shot across Atlantic Avenue running the lights. We couldn't. And lost him.

We came up with a plan for the next day. We knew he would stop at a certain location to pick up work. We had a car block the far end of the street. When he entered the area, we were right behind him. He took off, but soon saw he couldn't get through. He decided to back up, driving on the sidewalk! But, even with that, he couldn't make it out.

He was charged with slew of violations and was in tears when we vouchered his car. We did an exceptionally thorough job of looking for evidence.

No, we didn't break the back of organized crime.

But we gave them a headache.

DEATH OF AN INFORMANT

The tentacles of the original wiretap led us all over Brooklyn and Queens. There was an arrest made of a low-level thief named Charlie, who was caught breaking into a car. He mentioned that if the officers would give him a break he would tell them about an insurance scam. People were claiming their cars were stolen but, in reality, were told to drop it off at a junkyard, where it would be stripped of parts and eventually crushed for scrap.

You would never guess where this was all taking place. Right in the bar where we had the original tap!

I alerted our people to listen for any talk about insurance or cars. Within a few days, they heard a conversation from a male, who was asking Larry, the bartender, how to go about it.

"Leave the keys in the car," he said to the guy, "and the registration in case they get stopped." Larry told him where to park the car.

Since we had the description of the vehicle and its intended drop spot, we were there, watching, when they left it, got into a second car, and drove away.

We took pictures of the vehicle and, on the inside of the left front fender, we scratched the shield number of one of our officers.

We watched as the car was picked up and taken to the junkyard.

After a few days, the officer who had scratched his shield number on the fender, showed up at the junkyard and told one of the workers that he was looking for a left front fender for his car. He told him the year, model, etc.

The worker said he'd look around and shortly came back with a fender.

The officer looked it over, spotted his shield number and bought it.

The fender would be used as evidence when the cases were brought to trial.

Where, when, and how, we didn't know, but people found out that it was our thief, Charlie, who'd informed. We put him up in a hotel for safety reasons. But tough guy that he thought he was, Charlie called the bar and taunted Larry. He even challenged him to a fist fight. Larry laughed it off, telling him he had nothing against him and to come around and he'd buy him a drink.

They found Charlie dead, shot, early one morning when he went to visit his grandmother.

The whole office began to work on the information we got from wire taps including, loan sharking, insurance scams and threats made to anyone who received a subpoena.

One of the men on the team had to give a subpoena to a woman. When the husband opened the door, the officer said, "I have a subpoena."

The husband said, "I'll take it."

"No, it's for your wife."

"What?!"

In one day we issued over 140 subpoenas.

We continued to listen to the wiretap conversations and heard some people being warned about cooperating.

During the Grand Jury proceedings, a great many were asked questions such as, "Have you ever spoken to So-and-So?"

"No, I haven't."

"Thank you. You may leave."

When they left the Grand Jury room, the technician would play a tape of them talking to somebody, who warned them about testifying.

Many were charged with perjury.

So ended that investigation.

The unit was given a more difficult assignment. We were to gather evidence of a policy operation right in the heart of the Williamsburg section. It's a close-knit area, where families have lived since the Depression. Following someone on foot is almost impossible.

I personally knew the area, having lived there with my mom, two sisters, and my infant brother, during the time when my mom was telling us, "Your father won't be home for a few years." (You now know why.)

My family existed in those days with the help of a man whom, years later, I would be trying to put out of business and into jail.

As the investigation proceeded, there were times when my men thought they should operate the way we had before, with wiretaps, tailing people to pick up policy, etc. I told them to give it a shot.

There was a mountain of intelligence on that whole area, both from FBI, our department, State Police, the District Attorney's Office, and even the State Liquor Authority.

I wasn't disheartened. I knew what we were up against.

We went two ways.

The first was to have one of our men go to dinner with an attractive policewoman at either Bamontes or Cricis restaurant, so when they walked in, no one got uptight.

They had drinks at the bar in one place, then the other. It took a while, but this officer was good. I'll call him Bill. He was a good dresser, had a nice car—compliments of the department—and was a good tipper. Sure enough, they were invited for a drink at a table where some well-known people would usually show up. (He related how once, while he was sitting there, the singer, Jimmy Roselli, came by.)

We had our toe in the door. He let it be known, during his conversations with the bartenders and one waiter, that he had some "swag" in the trunk of his car. Leather jackets. Eventually, half of the club's employees were wearing leather jackets to work.

Bill seemed to be accepted as being an all right guy, but not by the people that mattered.

Not yet.

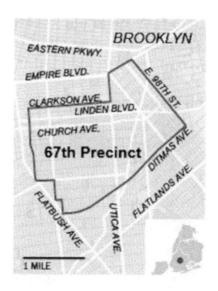

DUMPED BACK IN UNIFORM

Well, we had our toe in the door. My team was getting as cautious as I was. We didn't relish the idea of having one of us in a situation without backup.

Because of the policy arrest we'd made in the area, my face was known to both the bartender and to one particular waiter. I purposely dropped in from time to time, sat at the bar, ordered an anisette, and talked to the bartender.

After a while, the people in the bar area loosened up and stopped acting like they were in the ocean with a great white shark circling.

When I stopped in to eat with anyone from our office, I always told Armand the waiter, "Relax. We came to eat."

When doing so, we would occasionally peek to see who was sitting with Bill. We would return to the office and wait for Bill. Together we would update our files.

Way down the road, if Bill felt comfortable with those

people and they with him, he could feed them a story about making money. Our goal would be to borrow money, pay it back with the interest they demanded, borrow more, and then some more.

We talked to our bosses to get the go-ahead, letting them know it would be a slow process, and might result in indicting some of them.

In the meantime, relatives of mine were told by some of those who were involved in picking up policy, that they had seen me in the neighborhood. They asked, "Hey, how's he doing? Tell him to stop around the club when he gets a chance."

That was the overture.

I started to tiptoe around the neighborhood, making myself scarce. I didn't want to foul up the investigation.

The club they'd mentioned was on Metropolitan Avenue and Grand Street. Years ago, it was called Emil's. And, oh yeah, it was where Jimmy Nap used to do his business. He was number one on the FBI's hit parade. They've been trying to put him away for years. Eventually, years down the road, they made an arrest, due to extraordinary work by the FBI. They were motivated in their efforts by listening to Jimmy Nap's son badmouthing the FBI.

On one occasion, I was at Bamonte's having an anisette with one of my team. We knew our presence always shook people up. I was using the bathroom and in walked Jimmy Nap.

Damn, I thought. *This doesn't look good.*

I washed up, paid the bill, and we were out of there.

Once we were outside, I explained who Jimmy was, and told them it would be best not to be seen with him.

I found out that some people who knew my family were being told that certain people wanted to talk to me.

I figured that staying around this neighborhood wasn't doing the investigation any good.

Our normal hours were predicated on the hours that the bets were laid, the work was picked up, and deposited in the bank. It was imperative that any work collected after the last race was scrutinized. Woe to the guy who placed a bet after the last race and hit the number! They knew the consequences.

Once a month, we would work a 6 p.m. to 2 a.m. tour to answer complaints of prostitution, illegal after-hour clubs, etc. On April 27, 1976, we were scheduled for a 6 to 2 tour. Our team was discussing our investigation of loan sharking. There was a link between a bar in Manhattan and the people we were investigating.

I sent Bill to the Concord Bar and Grill on Lexington Avenue and East 32 Street with a backup team.

Lo and behold, the two lieutenants from our office were in the bar and grill.

Bill called me at the office and told me they were there.

I told him, "Leave after you identify the bartender."

The next day, when I showed up at ten, the two lieutenants were in the office with the inspector. (My blood is boiling as I write this.)

The inspector asked to see the log for the night before.

I showed him the log and entries regarding me sending Bill and his backup to the club. I asked the inspector, "Is this about me sending Bill to Manhattan?"

He had a blank look on his face.

He questioned the lieutenants.

They were in a bind, so the lies got bigger to save face.

"Well, we instructed you not to go there," they said.

I told them, "If you did, I don't remember. Nevertheless, it was a good tactic and if I thought it was good then, I think it was good now. Get the rope out."

They drew up papers with accusations. They transferred Bill back to patrol duty. They sent me to One Police Plaza while they figured out what they were going to do about me.

They gave me a desk to sit at.

An inspector instructed me to report to him when I went to the bathroom and when I went to meal!

I played their silly game for a few days.

They blinked first.

Every time the elevator opened, uniformed police officers, narcotic investigators, guys from the 23, guys from my old office, would all stop by and would shoot the breeze with me for a while.

I knew it was annoying the inspector.

He told me to report to another office in the Bronx, doing the same type of investigations that I'd been doing in Brooklyn. They had some good cases going. I would fit in fine.

On July 4, 1976, the other shoe fell.

I was to report in uniform to the 67 Precinct on Snyder Avenue in Brooklyn.

A dumping ground.

WAKING THE DEAD

Well, I almost had my 20 years in, so I decided to suck it up, do my time, and milk the job until I retired.

Who was I kidding? That never was my style.

I told my wife about my transfer. We had been through so much together, that I couldn't let her see how much it affected me.

She got out my shirts and started to iron them. I was to report and do a midnight to 8 a.m. starting that night!

When I reported for my first tour, I saw that there was no inspection of uniforms or the men by the desk officer.

Not a good sign.

I was the patrol supervisor for that tour. The sergeant's driver was six feet, two inches tall, a guy named Al Ross, "Big Al" to everyone. And lo and behold, he was the same Big Al who had been best man for my cousin, Donald, when he'd married beautiful Susan.

Donald was a detective in the narcotics division, well-decorated. But I remember when he was 16 and bullied by a kid in his high school.

He had come to my basement apartment and asked me, "What should I do?"

I'd been on the job about a year, and he always looked up to me. I couldn't let him down. The kid, who'd been bullying him, wanted to fight him in a ring at the YMCA on Nostrand Avenue.

We went to my parents' house and put on a pair of boxing gloves that my brother and I used for sparring.

Once Donald got hit in the face a couple of times, the fear went out of him.

We went to the YMCA, and after the first round, the bully quit.

Big Al was a soft-spoken guy and after talking about my transfer for a while, we got a call of a street fight on Flatbush Avenue.

When we got there, another sector car was trying to calm things down. Big Al and I got out. I took my nightstick with me. When I put up my hands to push people back, someone grabbed my night stick, probably thinking I was going to hit him.

I yanked it back and felt something give in my shoulder.

Big Al must have seen the look on my face. He grabbed that guy and was using his face for a hood ornament.

Everyone took off. No arrests.

I got back in the car.

"Do you want to go to the hospital?" Al asked me.

"Heck, no. First tour here and I go sick? Not a good precedent."

I kept my thoughts and opinions to myself during the first few days at the 67.

It was like two precincts in one. One group, hard workers doing everyday tasks. The others, slackers and drinkers.

Later, I found out that they'd been dumped in that precinct from elsewhere, and they gravitated together.

On one occasion, during a 4 p.m. to midnight tour, they used the car radios to coordinate a meeting at a cemetery. I showed up and did them a big favor by telling them to get back on patrol and ditch the beer bottles.

They repaid me by putting toothpicks in my car locks.

I let it be known that I'd break up the teams, which would have screwed up their carpooling. They relented.

During my stay at the 67, I was able to recruit some card players to our Thursday night game. (What?! You never heard of our card game? My gosh, it's been going on since 1969! Let me look back some pages to see if I mentioned it before. Wow! How did that happen?)

Let me see, there was Big Al, Anthony "Blinky" Incarbone, John Costello, Jack Sherman, Paul Lyden, Eddie Shull, Patty Vadala, and a few more I can't remember. We played on Thursday, because that was pay day. One night, Big Al lost his temper and turned over the table, and when he left our club, he tore the door off its hinges. *That* was exciting!

Let's get back to police work....

My driver was John Sapienza, a good guy, young and eager to learn. We got a call of a possible DOA.

We were met there by the sector concerned and the landlady. She told us the man, who rented her upstairs apartment, hadn't answered his door, and water was dripping down into her kitchen.

We climbed the stairs and knocked on his door. We could hear a radio.

She didn't have a key, so we got her permission to force the door.

We called for Emergency Service, as they had the tools.

They arrived and tried to force the lock.

I think they put too much pressure on the frame and, not only did the door give in, but the whole frame tore loose and came crashing down into the kitchen!

There was a dog in the apartment who ran away into another room, and we didn't see it until we left.

There was that old, familiar, smell of rotten flesh.

The sink was loaded with dishes and pots with the faucet dripping and overflowing.

We walked into the bedroom, all seven of us—my driver, the landlady, the two from the sector car, the two Emergency Services officers and myself.

We were standing at the foot of the bed. The body was under the covers, and there was a radio playing softly by his bed. The music wasn't necessary and a little annoying.

I said, "John, shut the radio off."

He reached over and turned it off.

The instant he did, our "dead" body sat up in bed!

What?!

A while later, when we started to leave, the landlady shouted, "What about the door?"

We kept walking. We advised her to put in a claim with the city, and we left.

As it turned out, the stink was some rotten meat in the garbage.

When John and I got into the car, we laughed, and I said, "That's the first thing you're going to talk about when you go home."

TWO RUNAWAYS

Desk duty can be hectic if you haven't got the temperament. We would all like the tour to begin with a clean slate. It doesn't work that way.

There were things to be accounted for before you wrote anything in the log book. An inventory had to be entered after you verified that all the property vouched was secure in the property locker. Entries were made on any changes in the original roll call. These were just mundane things that any desk officer handled every tour.

I was doing a 4 p.m. to midnight tour as the desk officer, and it was going smoothly.

My tour was almost over, and the fire department came in with a young boy who'd been left alone in a house that had a minor fire. I remember the child had an unusual name.

The clerical staff took the information and called social services. The boy would be turned over to them, until the parents either reported him missing or picked him up from wherever social service had deposited him.

Everything was handled almost perfectly. Unfortunately, the clerical staff neglected to instruct Missing Persons Bureau: If anyone inquires for the whereabouts of this boy, let them know where he was sent by social services.

This was a big boo-boo on their part and a disaster for the desk officer.

When I showed up for work the next tour, there was chaos. Hundreds of officers were being assigned to different blocks.

I made it through the crowd to the desk, which had been taken over by all kinds of brass.

I pulled the deck officer aside. I still was in civilian clothes, as I wasn't on duty yet. He mentioned something about a missing boy and mumbled the kids' name.

Yikes!

I told him that the FD had brought him in last night, and we had notified social services. We told the desk officer where they'd sent the boy.

He was ecstatic and informed the duty captain where the child was. The duty captain passed the word up the ladder. They started to dismiss the officers back to their command.

Everything calmed down.

I took the clerical civilian aside and told him to make an entry that Missing Persons had been notified.

A lie?

Who knows?

All's well that ends well.

The procedure that's used today came about in the early 1960s. Now, if there is a missing child reported, and officers are directed to check every apartment that is assigned to them, they are required to physically enter and search the premises. Any locked apartment is noted and will be visited again.

I'll never forget one missing persons case we had at the 67 Precinct. I was doing a 4 p.m. to midnight tour when we received a call that two sisters were missing.

They'd been playing at a friend's apartment. Since the next day was a school day, the girls, ages 12 and 13, had said their goodbyes and left for home.

My driver was Anthony "Blinky" Incarbone, one of our Thursday night poker players. I enjoyed riding with him. He was a good guy, and we used to sing in the car to pass the time. We did a particularly rousing version of the old spiritual, "Let My People Go." I don't know how in tune we were, but we were loud. Very loud.

Anyway, we were the first to interview the parents of the girls they had been playing with at the time.

It was late and when we knocked, the father answered and came out in the hall to talk to us. He said his children were already in bed.

I told him, "It's important that we ask the kids a few questions."

He let us inside, and we spoke to the girls quietly.

They said the missing girls hadn't really intended to go home. "Their parents didn't know," they told us. "Please, don't tell them!"

We got the name and address of the friend the girls were going to see.

Then we thanked the father and left.

We notified Central where we'll be and why.

Our tour had ended minutes before. I asked my driver if he wanted to go back to the house. "Heck no," he said. "Let's see where this takes us."

We arrived at the address. The apartment the girls were going to visit was on the sixth floor.

We knocked, knocked, and knocked some more. Finally, a man opened the door, and I quickly explained why we were there.

He said he knew who the girls were and told us they'd left a while ago.

We thanked him.

We were walking to the elevator when Anthony said, "Wait a minute. I'm going to check the roof."

He ran up, while I waited.

Then I heard him yell, "Sarge! Come here!"

Under the stairwell leading to the roof, there they were, hugging each other and softly sobbing.

Anthony spoke quietly to them, calmed them down.

It all was about some nonsense in school, and they were afraid of being disciplined by their parents.

Only God knows what could have happened to those kids.

Rather than take them home, we brought them to the station house first, then notified the parents.

Thank you, Anthony Incarbone!

DEATH OF A GOOD COP

Cecile Sledge. Ever hear of him? If you'd been with Eddie Shull and me on January 28, 1980, and had seen what we saw, you'd never forget that name.

Eddie and I were doing a 4 p.m. to midnight tour in the 67 Precinct. Eddie and I had been in the same class in the academy, back in 1957. (Wow, seems like a long time ago.)

I was the patrol sergeant, and Eddie was assigned as the operator. I remember it was cold winter night.

We were about to notify Central that we'd be out of service for meal, when we heard a hysterical voice, screaming into his mike.

Central was trying to have him repeat his message.

Other voices came on the air. Also hysterical.

We were able to make out a street name in the 69 Precinct. I told Eddie, "Let's get over there."

We pulled into the street just in time to see officers, some in uniform and others in civilian clothes, hustle someone into the back seat of an unmarked department car and speed away.

When we got out of our car, we realized we were the only uniformed officers around.

On the sidewalk across from us lay an aluminum light, knocked down somehow, and a horribly mangled body.

There was an ambulance attendant nearby. I asked him what happened. All he said was, "That's a cop!"

Police Officer Cecile Sledge's life had come to an end on January 28, 1980, by being dragged under a car for about a half a mile.

Eddie and I couldn't digest what we are looking at. God, was he alive while being dragged?

Later, I'd pray that he'd died in the exchange of gunfire with the lowlife he'd been trying to arrest.

The guy they were hustling into the unmarked police was Salvatore DeSarno. He was tried, convicted, and sentenced to life imprisonment.

Eddie and I stuck it out, until we were relieved, sometime around 3 a.m.

When I got home, my wife was awake, waiting for me. I just told her that some cop got killed and held her real tight.

There are dangers and sometime violent deaths awaiting police officers, fireman, and anyone we now call "first responders."

No one in his right mind thinks that anything is going to happen to him. But sometimes it does, doesn't it?

Did Sergeant Edward Johnson think he would be stabbed to death in a flop house on the Bowery? Did my buddy Vincent Zichetella imagine he'd be shot to death effecting an arrest on the Penn Station taxi ramp? How could Detective Anthony Campisi have known he'd be stabbed by a pimp while arresting a prostitute, something he has done many times before?

I mention these because I either knew them or watched them die in an emergency room.

But I'll tell you about a death that no one can explain except our Maker.

I was called to a one-family house in Canarsie, the home of a police officer and his wife, who were expecting their first child. We were met out front by another officer who stated that he and the cop who lived there were scheduled to appear at the Grand Jury to give information on an arrest they had both participated in.

His partner had been unduly worried because, at the time of the arrest, they'd let a couple of people leave the scene.

When the officer we were talking to had come to pick up his partner, so they could ride to court together, he'd found guy's pregnant wife crying uncontrollably.

She'd been making breakfast when she'd heard a shot from upstairs.

Her husband had shot himself to death with his service revolver.

Can anyone explain *that* to me?

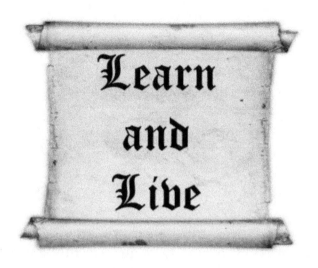

COMPLAINT NUMBER TWO

The 67 Precinct was a mixture of busy areas of stores, bodegas, auto repair shops and residences. All were fair game for burglars, robbers, and those who commented acts of violence of all kinds.

On one particular busy day, a unit got a call of gunfire in the basement of an apartment house. I let Central know, "We're also responding."

When we got there, we found the other unit already in the basement.

"Nothing here, Sarge," they told me.

I would have agreed with this officer, except I'd known him to be a slacker and besides, I smelled cordite. (Fancy for gun smoke.)

Sure enough, we found a body behind some washing machines. It was a male. He couldn't have been dead too long.

We secured the area and let Central know what we had.

We told them to notify the 67 Squad.

One of our Thursday night poker players, Detective Pasquale Vidalia showed up. But before he could begin his investigation, we received another call from Central about a shooting in front of the very building we were in!

We hurried back up to the street and sure enough there was another male, shot dead, lying by the curb.

"Good luck, Paddy. I'll see you Thursday at the game," I told Pasquale.

I left a few uniformed men there to assist in crowd control.

We resumed patrol and shortly received a call of a burglary in progress. We got there just as the sector assigned showed up. I did what you would see on TV. I sent them to the rear.

The back door had been forced. They let us in through the front door.

They had two terrified teenagers already in cuffs.

These two police officers were the ones I'd confronted in a cemetery with beer and, keeping true to form, one of them punched a kid who was crying in the chest.

I took the officer aside and told him, "If I ever see you do that again, I'll bring charges against you."

The occupants showed up, an elderly couple. They were petrified at the sight of so many people in their house. My driver was talking to them.

I asked the two who responded to check the house.

One of them went upstairs, came back down, and said, "It looks all right."

As we were leaving, the gentleman let out a yell and pointed to the closet. There was another kid hiding in the closet, not five feet from where we were talking!

Live and learn.

That expression should be, "Learn and Live!"

We returned to the station house, close to the end of the

tour, when Big Al was pumping gas. He had that job until he retired. He called me over and said, "We have a new CO."

He'd heard from cops under this captain's previous command that he was a disciplinarian.

I thought to myself, *Good luck with that*.

When I was about to sign out in the blotter, the clerical civilian said to me, "The captain wants to see you in his office."

I knocked and walked in.

"Sergeant Cocalas," he said.

"Captain."

"Sergeant, you are behind on the communications you were assigned. Close them out by the end of the week."

"Okay, Captain."

I left and thought to myself, *Big Al was right*.

I hated those complaints, made by various cross sections of the community—noise, loitering in front of the church, etc. They were time consuming, and you had to fudge a bit to close them out.

"Did you see any violations?"

"No."

"Did you speak to the complainant?"

"Yes."

"How many times did you visit the location?"

"Never. Oops! I mean four thousand seventy times."

(Just kidding.)

I was lucky and completed the complaints that were assigned to me.

Not so for a sergeant who was on the lieutenants' list to be promoted soon. That captain gave him some complaints to be investigated. The sergeant turned them in the next day with some stated, "Unfounded."

The captain assigned the integrity sergeant to verify the findings. The integrity sergeant could have given the sergeant a heads up.

Instead, that sergeant was brought up on charges, found guilty and passed over when his list number on the lieutenants' list was reached.

He wasn't taken off the list, but he had to wait until the next group was promoted—maybe months, maybe years.

Well, then it came my turn to lock horns with the captain.

I was working a day tour, an 8 a.m. to 4 p.m., when we heard a call of a burglary in progress in an apartment, no more than a block from where we were.

My driver was anxious to make this arrest, and he did.

We caught this creep coming out of the building we were headed for. Another car pulled up, and my driver said, "I got this."

They took the suspect to the station house.

We got the superintendent to secure the apartment, and we returned to the house.

My driver was filling out the arrest report and wouldn't have been available for the rest of the tour.

I picked up the officer who had station house security and went back on patrol.

It was past my scheduled meal time so I transmitted to Central, "67 sergeant taking a delayed meal."

He replied, "Ten four, 67 sergeant taking a delayed meal."

Later, that reply would be music to my ears, when I was in the trial room.

We were in a restaurant when we heard, "1013." (An officer needs assistance.)

We left our meal and went to the location where the cop needed help.

When we got there, I saw a radio car with one officer standing alongside it. The team that had called the 1013 said the radio car wasn't necessary. I had them resume patrol.

Then I turned to the remaining officer, one of the slackers from the cemetery episode.

I asked him, "Where's your partner?"

Before he answered, a cab pulled up and the other slacker showed up. Said he was on a personal.

"Bull," I said, "I'll talk to you two later. Now get on patrol."

That incident spread throughout the precinct wash women and, sure enough, the captain heard about it. He called the two into his office and interviewed them.

He gave them a choice. "Go to the Trial Room with formal charges or take command discipline and lose two days' vacation."

They took the loss of the two days.

The next day, I was called to his office, and he related some cock and bull story that the slackers gave him, placing the blame on me, and he offered me command discipline of loss of five vacation days or the trial room.

I said, "I'll take the trial room."

He was shocked. He wrote up a list of violations, and I was served with them. A date with the trial room had to be determined, and I would be told when.

I thought, *Doesn't that SOB know I'm on the lieutenants' list?*

You bet he did.

The time came for me to go to the trial room. They read the charges. Before I pled, I advised my appointed lawyer to subpoena the radio transmitting for that day.

That sweet voice came over loud and clear, "Ten-four, 67 sergeant taking a delayed meal."

In their haste to crush me, they were saying they had me for failing to respond at such and such time. When I first read the original charge typed up, I knew they had the times screwed up. If I'd corrected them, there and then, all they'd have had to do was type it over and change the time.

After that, I had to tiptoe and stay out of trouble. Our

beloved captain was transferred to the 9 Precinct. They had a discipline problem and knew he was a disciplinarian.

Talk about Karma.

The day the results from my trial came, our fine captain walked in the door. I ripped open the envelope and on the last page I read: Charge #1—Not Guilty, Charge #2—Not Guilty, Charge #3—Not Guilty.

I walked over to him and held up the third page to him.

"Oh. Good for you, Jim," he said.

That hypocrite!

Within a day or so, I got the word I was to be promoted. The clerical sergeant from the borough office said he was trying to get me a certain easy precinct. I thanked him and said, "I'll take whatever fate has in store for me."

I was promoted to lieutenant shortly after that.

PROMOTION TO LIEUTENANT

Making lieutenant, believe me I'm not bragging, was an accomplishment for me personally. How could I be bragging? It took me two lieutenant tests and twenty-four years to finally get promoted.

Did I feel like Cagney on those gas tanks yelling, "Top of the world!?" Yes, I did. Did you see the next scene when it all blows up in his face? That couldn't happen to me, could it? Read on.

I brought Barbara with me to the ceremony. That was a great day. The sergeant I mentioned earlier, who was going to get me a good precinct...he did. But I just didn't like to tempt fate.

I was assigned the 61 on Coney Island Avenue. It's in a residential area with high income homes and the affluent people to go with them.

The residents were very influential. So much so that, when the precinct was being built, they insisted that the concept of a large desk with a rail in front of it was taboo. They wanted it replaced with a regular side business type desk. They insisted that said desk would be placed about ten feet in front of the entrance!

Every other office was behind that desk, including the muster room, where the sergeants or the commanding officer would turn out the platoon.

An obvious fault was, if an officer made an arrest, he would enter through the rear doors. The desk officer wouldn't know about the arrest, such as the condition of the prisoner, the charge, anything to be vouchered, etc. I made these observations within the first hour. And within that first hour one of the inside police officers came around and asked for a contribution so they could buy the outgoing captain a gift of a hunting rifle. I thought, *What is this,* The Andy Griffith Show*? Is this Mayberry? Where's Opey?*

I introduced myself around. I met the soon-to-be-gone captain. He seemed like a pleasant enough man. Who wouldn't have been, leaving this command with a hunting rifle as a going away gift?

It was hard for me to digest what a laidback place that was to work. What made it even easier was...they gave the lieutenant, who had desk duty, two options. He could go on patrol in a sector car. Or he could stay in the station house and sit ten feet in front of the door to await a complaint by a 75-year-old woman who said the local deli didn't give her the right change. Or better still, wait for a psycho to come roaring in with not one uniformed officer in sight.

Yes, I'm exaggerating, but you get the idea. Which would you take, sit at that desk or have someone drive you around and maybe see the boats come in at Sheepshead Bay? And what made it better was that they had a lieutenant who volunteered to do steady late tours!

On a quiet day, a unit was called to an apartment building to meet the parents of a daughter who lived there. They hadn't been able to reach her by phone and felt something must be wrong. They had gone to her home and, when no one answered their knocks, they let themselves in and found their daughter lying naked on the floor.

The unit called for a supervisor. I responded and spoke to the parents, who stated they hadn't gone in when they'd seen their daughter lying on the floor.

We went to the apartment and discovered a nude female lying face down, apparently dead, with a hemp-type rope around her neck.

The detectives responded and immediately questioned me as to how many officers had entered the room. They deemed this to be a homicide and a crime scene.

I give them credit. They were efficient and, after talking to the parents, they found out she was seeing a police officer on occasion.

A few weeks later, I spoke to one of the detectives, and he revealed this boyfriend and the woman were sexually involved and in the course of them experimenting, she had succumbed.

Imagine the parents!

BAD RUMORS

Do you know the meaning of the word "paradox?" I thought I did, and after I looked it up in the dictionary, I realized that's what we had in the 61 Precinct. It was, by and far, the quietest precinct I'd worked in. Yet we had an officer assigned there who made more overtime than anyone else in the whole city.

The *Daily News* did a series on overtime in various services supplied to the city. Whether it was transit, sanitation, fire department, etc., we came up with the champ! New as I was to the precinct, someone pointed him out to me at the most opportune time.

I was on patrol, riding around my old neighborhood and bending my driver's ear.

"Hey, there's Dubrow's. I used to eat there. There's the Avalon movie. Did I ever tell you how we snuck in there?" And so on.

As we were driving up Kings Highway, I noticed a group of youths, hanging out under the BMT between East 15 and East 16. I glanced over and, in doing so, I saw one of them giving me the finger.

"Stop the car!"

I jumped out, and the kid didn't know whether to run or play macho man and stand his ground. He ran, right in the arms of the 61 cop with the most overtime in the city. He'd been in an unmarked department car, responding to a report of a disorderly group.

When we got back to the precinct, the washerwomen knew all about it.

It boosted my standings, as you can imagine.

That news story didn't put a damper on that officer.

To prevent him from making arrests, thus cut down his overtime, they assigned him to drive the duty captain of the division to the precincts in the borough.

It didn't work.

En route to one of the precincts, he observed someone stripping a car. They had just about finished the job.

The officer pulled over, and the captain asked him what he was doing.

"Cap, he's stripping that car, and I'm going to arrest him."

"Listen, forget it," the captain said, "and take me to the precinct."

"Okay, Captain. Let me put this in my memo book."

The captain had stepped in it and knew he was defeated.

He told his driver to have another car respond. When they did, he told them to make the arrest.

They would have, except the driver–whom the captain was supposed to prevent from making any overtime–spoke up. "This is my collar. I observed the violation."

The captain told one of the responding officers, "Take me to the Borough Office." He did and went back to pick up the officer and his prisoner. He won that round and try as they might, they couldn't stop him.

The washerwomen knew about it before he got back from court. He was known to make arrests on his way from the courthouse. He was certainly more courageous than I was.

There was an undercurrent of an impending investigation in the precinct. I was pretty good at ferreting out information from cops. I played cards with them while off duty or had coffee with them, sitting in a radio car, shooting the breeze. No dice.

There was talk about the officer with the most OT being the subject of the investigation, but try as they might, nothing would stick to him. They didn't lay a glove on him (an old boxing term). But the rumors continued.

During this time, I was approached by a police officer, who drove me a couple of times. He told me he was putting in his papers (retiring), and I asked him why. He just put his twenty years in and couldn't give me a reason. I asked him if it was about the rumors going around. He just shook his head.

It all came to a boiling point in a few months. It surprised me, the stupidity of it all. And it all came about just as I thought it would, when I saw the way the construction of the precinct was set up. All they had to do was to ask a "dinosaur," but the brains didn't trust them with these younger officers.

Well, they paid for it in bad publicity for the department. The worst was yet to come.

TRANSFER TO 69 PRECINCT

We got a new commanding officer in the 61, a young man who I thought they, meaning the brass, were grooming for deputy and, after that, the sky's the limit. I could never find out who "they" were.

Way back, when I was in the 14 Precinct and my partner was Bob Mullany, we got a call back to the house to pick up an inspector. He got in the passenger's, and I was relegated to the back seat. No problem.

He went to various precincts and made an entry, so they would know he was around. (There's that "they" again.)

When he got back in the car, I lit up a cigarette.

Without turning his head, the inspector said, "Douse that cigarette. They don't like us smoking in public."

I thought, *Let me get this straight. It's 3 in the morning. He's a full inspector. There's probably a half dozen people on the streets at this hour.* (We didn't have drones in those days.)

When I was on the USS Midway, and they were refueling planes, I could see it. They would say over the loud speaker, "The smoking lamp is out during refueling." I knew who "they" were.

I looked behind us while Bob was driving. Nope, nobody following us. I told myself, *Forget it. Concentrate on what's going on in the precinct.*

I took the desk that fateful day.

In walked an individual in civilian clothes, who I had pegged as a boss, and I was so right.

"Can I help you, sir?"

"I'm Inspector So-and-So."

(You sure you're not called Sourpuss?)

"Get rid of that cobblestone holding the door open," he said. "Somebody is going to trip on that."

HUH?

The first officer I saw, I told him, "Officer, remove that cobblestone. Somebody may trip on it."

He says, "HUH?"

I shook my head, not knowing Sourpuss was still standing there. He disappeared into the labyrinth behind me.

In about five minutes, our new captain comes out to my desk and inquires of me, "What did you say to the inspector, Lieutenant?"

"Huh?"

"He said you have a bad attitude."

"Cap, he told me to remove the cobblestone that's been holding the door open as long as I've been here."

"I'm only telling you what he said."

Well, I didn't think anything of it and continued my normal schedule.

After a few days I was notified, not by the captain but by a clerical sergeant, that I was transferred to the 69 Precinct effective 0800 tomorrow.

HUH?

It was a blessing in disguise. Shortly after I was transferred, that investigation in the 61 Precinct ended, and it was a blockbuster! A sergeant and three officers were suspended to await criminal charges.

It seems that there was a broken window in a local haberdasher and the four took shirts, etc., and were dropping them off in their private vehicles in the precinct parking lot.

The sergeant and his driver went back to make sure there wasn't a video on the premises. They reentered the building and went to the basement...where members of Internal Affairs awaited them.

Those charged didn't include our overtime guy at all. Good for him.

I don't throw stones or gloat over the fact that I knew what was bound to happen.

As an offshoot of this tragedy, they eventually reconstructed the interior. Now the desk officer has knowledge of all that occurs inside the station house. He has a view of the muster room, the rear doors to the parking lot, the stairwell, the clerical staff, and the entrance.

I felt like there was a cloud following me from place to place. There I was, going to a new precinct, the 69 in Canarsie. Little did I know that there was an active investigation going on involving superior officers.

Give me a break!

SUICIDE WHILE IN CUSTODY

I know Canarsie from the days when I worked at that skeet shooting club close to where the Belt Parkway is now, way back in ancient times, the late 1940s.

There were "squatters" living between the Belt and about two or three hundred yards inland. They strung wires to the Belt's electric system and tapped into their light poles. Some real tough people.

They constructed shacks and, to overcome the sometime damp, mushy ground, they laid planks down to go from place to place.

Eventually, the city made a move and got them evicted.

I think some of that toughness is still in the people of Canarsie.

When I showed up at the station house, I recognized some of the cops from being on details with them and the funeral of Cecil Sledge. The captain, lieutenants, and sergeants were friendly and were well aware of what had gone down in the 61 Precinct.

I found out later that the lieutenant who did steady late tours in the 61 had been promoted to captain and sadly, because of the scandal, and because he was still on probation, they dumped him back a rank to lieutenant! Wow!

The 69 Precinct was a combination of small businesses, homes, a few large apartment buildings close to the Belt, a scrap metal area (junkyards), a large food terminal, and some industry.

Luckily, they still had the concept of the lieutenant being the tour commander. Most of my time was spent riding in a sector car, responding to jobs, giving assistance when needed, and in general, keeping the men on their toes.

The people, who lived in that area, seemed friendlier than the other precincts I'd worked in. I really think that the death of Cecil Sledge had bonded the police and the community.

There was an incident that, later, became a tragedy for a family.

One weekend evening, the sector car came into the station house with a young man in custody.

A while back, long before I had arrived there, he had been arrested for a minor offence on the complaint of a young lady, possibly his girlfriend. He had been incarcerated, and in the system, he could earn weekend furlough.

According to the arresting officers, he had approached this woman again, and she made another complaint.

He was arrested and placed in a holding cell, which was to the left of the desk. They handcuffed one of his hands to a holding bar while they completed their paper work and told the sergeant on the desk they were going back to notify the parents that their son has been arrested again. They had dealt with this young man before. There was a security window so anyone assigned desk duty could watch the prisoner. On this tour, a sergeant was assigned desk duty.

My driver and I were on our meal hour. There was a lounge in the basement and I was watching a football game on TV. The civilian switchboard operator rushed downstairs and rattled off something that I couldn't understand.

"Slow down," I said. "What's the matter?"

I made out, "...sergeant, prisoner...." So, I ran up to the desk.

The sergeant was in the holding cell, trying to remove the laces that the prisoner had tied around his own neck!

The cell door only opened from the outside. I made sure not to close it.

We managed to get the laces off his neck, but I knew he was dead.

Well, there was nothing we could do, so I told the sergeant to start making notifications.

We had to inform the 69 squad, the duty captain, our captain, and the medical examiners' office.

And since the cells in station houses are the jurisdiction of the Correction Department, they had to be notified, too.

I spoke to the Correction Department representative, and he must have known I was upset about the prisoner killing himself. He explained how it was done and also told me the methods used in prison. What this young man had done was...loosen the laces on the sneakers, loop them over his neck, tie the other ends to the bar and slide down, but not completely off the seat. His weight put tightening pressure on the carotid arteries causing him first to pass out and then eventually die.

It wouldn't have taken long.

Anybody glancing at him wouldn't have thought anything was wrong.

I felt so bad, both for this troubled young man and for the sergeant who had attempted to save him.

The investigation didn't point the finger at anyone.

There was only one more task that had to be done.

Inform the family.

I took it upon myself to notify them.

My driver and I went to their apartment and knocked. The father answered.

When he saw us, he said, "Yeah, we know he got arrested again. The other officer told us."

"Sir," I said. "Can we come in? I have some bad news." We went inside. I told him, "Your son killed himself in the station house."

He stepped back into the room. His wife was lying on a couch. It looked like she was sleeping. "Get up!" he yelled at her. "Get up! They killed our boy!"

He ran out, went to another apartment, and was banging on the door. He told someone about his son.

The next thing I knew, the neighbor came charging at me and crowded me against a cabinet. We had to restrain him. I quickly filled him in on what had happened.

Other people came in, and he quietly explained it all to them.

We told them how sorry we were about what had happened, and then we left.

I thought to myself, *Why me, Lord? When I get home will my wife sense any change in me?*

TRANSFERS AND CHARGES FOR ALL

A couple of things happened that were a little unusual in the 69. One being the robbery of a jewelry store owner, as he was getting on the Belt Parkway from the marina that juts out from the Belt. They forced his car over and robbed him of a case he was carrying.

No injuries, so it became a case for the detective squad. We took all the information, turned it over to the squad, and I had the sectors resume patrol.

It was unusual in that it was done on the parkway with traffic moving right along and no rubber necking.

The other was a stick-up of a bodega, where one of the workers was shot in the face, but not killed.

I responded, and it was hard to believe. The bullet knocked out his front tooth.

He was sitting on the floor, leaning against the shelves, awaiting an ambulance, and the sector was getting information from the owners. I looked the guy over and there were no other wounds him. Had to be the caliber of the gun used. He should have had a lethal wound but no, he was just sitting there.

Here is the other unusual part of this robbery. The store had plastic bottles of sodas along the wall where the worker was sitting. I noticed one of the plastic bottles was "fizzing." I looked closely at it and, lo and behold, there in that plastic soda bottle was the bullet that had knocked his tooth out.

We all were amazed, including the detectives when they showed up.

Since there was nothing more for us or the sector to do, we resumed patrol. The sector gave Central all the info they had about the suspect to be broadcast to other sectors.

I thought I'd gotten rid of the black cloud that had been following me from my last two commands.

Wrong!

Internal Affairs had been following two police officers in the 69 Precinct that were assigned to executing warrants on people who hadn't appeared at court when their cases were called.

They were given an unmarked car and special hours. After serving the arrest warrant, they would take the subject to court. Easy enough, wouldn't you think?

In fact, the warrants were for non-violent cases such as misdemeanor possession of drugs, failure to show in simple assault cases and other quality of life offenses.

The investigators found that, after they'd made an arrest, one would take that individual to court, and the other would go home, or attend to the private businesses they both had.

On the next arrest, they would reverse rolls. The one who went to court would come back to the station house and sign both of them out.

I have no doubt that someone in the command informed Internal Affairs.

The rest of the command continued to do what was required of them. The shoe hadn't dropped yet, and when it finally did, all the bosses—sergeants, lieutenants and the captain—were affected by it.

The precinct was still doing their job, responding to accidents, attending to people who needed an ambulance at their home, protecting property at night, and making arrests when called for. We even got the opportunity to have a softball game after us old timers were challenged. (I would like to say we won, but I think we lost. I was the manager for the old timers.)

Well, after thinking, *I wouldn't mind spending the rest of my "career" here and maybe start studying for captain*, they dropped the first shoe. The two officers were suspended. I don't think they were arrested but were made to pay some sort of restitution such as loss of vacation days or monetary loss.

And, of course, they investigated all who had desk duty during the times those guys had pulled their scheme. This included the captain, who eventually lost his command.

The borough office called each of us individually to give testimony. We had a representative from our line organization present. No decisions would be made in the hearings until all who were involved had been interviewed.

My turn came. I was sitting at a table with a representative from the lieutenants' association seated at my left.

It began.

"While you were the tour commander, you were the supervisor over the two officers now under suspension, correct."

"Partially."

Wham, my rep nudges my knee. He was letting me know, wrong answer.

"Explain that, lieutenant."

"Well, the two officers start their tour at 6 a.m. I start my day tour at 7:10 a.m."

Wham, another nudge by my rep.

I continued, "They' re assigned an unmarked car and are permitted to leave the precinct. I'm in a marked department car, performing duties assigned to me by Central. Their tour is over at 2 p.m. Mine is done at 3:15. In truth, I rarely see them, even during the other tours."

That was where they got me with my pants down. "Next time you're called," they said, "bring your memo books."

Great. I hadn't made an entry in months.

The interviews were over and their decision was as follows: The captain lost his command, the four lieutenants were transferred within the borough, three sergeants were transferred within the borough.

I was home, awaiting a call.

The phone rang, and my wife picked it up. "Jim," she said, "it's Paulie." (He was one of my card players, who was also a sergeant in the borough office.)

I took the phone. "Yo, Paulie. What's up?"

"You're getting transferred. "

"Yeah, I know," I said, thinking it would be some precinct in the borough. "Where to?"

"The 28."

Years later, Bobbie told me that I turned white.

CHAOS IN THE CELLS

I was really disheartened, but I never let Barbara see how discouraged I was. Harlem. The dreaded 28 Precinct. At that time the smallest precinct in the city. The precinct where Police Officer Phil Cardillo was killed in a mosque. It was the precinct where Fidel Castro stayed at the Theresa Hotel, and where I got knocked on my butt during a riot.

Most of clientele in that precinct had no love for the police, and confrontations arose, even with the issuing of traffic summons.

That was running around my head as I was driving there for my first tour.

I pulled into the parking lot, got my gear, and heard my father say, "Head high, Jim."

I entered, and at the desk was a lieutenant named A. J. Matthews. He was a large, black man with a big friendly smile. He got me in a bear hug and said, "Welcome to the 28, Jim."

He bought me upstairs to meet the clerical staff run by Miss Sandy, another kindly black person with a sweet soul, who invited respect. I never called her anything but "Miss Sandy" all the time I was there. (Her husband was Randy Sandy. If you follow the fight game, you probably know he was a referee in professional bouts at Madison Square Garden.)

I found out that the former commanding officer and his integrity officer were sent to the 69 Precinct to fill in the vacancies that were left after that disaster caused by those two selfish (Can I say bastards?) officers.

I went down to the desk and introduced myself. Officer Mike Greene assisted the desk officer, mostly by acting as a buffer between the desk officer and the public. Then there was Officer Bobby DeLoose, a former lieutenant in the U. S. Army, who served in Vietnam. In addition to clerical duties assigned him, he fingerprinted everyone brought into the station under arrest.

The precinct had a narcotics unit called SNEU comprised of police officers in civilian clothes that effected many of the drug arrests in the precinct. There was a safe for storing any narcotics brought in, until a unit from the police lab came to remove them.

Being close to that safe, you would get a whiff of something new on the market called "angel dust."

In a few words, this place was busy,

It had detention cells for about twenty prisoners, which other station houses sometimes used when their own cells were overcrowded.

I told you it was busy!

During a day tour, an officer came to the desk. His name was Gene Entel. He was assigned summons duty on West 125. He said the sector car was bringing in his prisoner.

I got to know Gene over the years at the 28 Precinct. He hadn't a mean bone in his body. (Dare I use the word "meek?") He said he was writing a parking ticket for a car when the owner showed up and caused a crowd to collect. It almost turned physical when a sector car showed up and Gene was forced to arrest the owner of the car.

And here they came into the station house. Two officers struggling with Gene's prisoner. I directed them to the cells, and they deposited him there.

"Entel, give me some info on this guy," I said, "so I can make an entry in the log."

Gene went into the cell area and came right back out. "He said he's going to kill me."

No sense explaining to Gene that the guy was in a cell, and the cell was in a police station.

I spotted Sgt. John Quinn and said to him, "Do me a favor and give Entel a hand."

At that time, the wagon showed up to take prisoners downtown. I told them, "Hold on. We'll have one for you in a minute."

Entel came out of the cell area. "Lieutenant, he's giving the sarge a hard time."

"Bobby, find out what the hell is going on in there," I said, "Police Officer Gallagher, give Bobby a hand in the cells."

Entel comes running out again with Sergeant Quinn. "Lieutenant, you better call an ambulance! That jerk tried to run past us and cracked his head on the cell door!"

I'd been there before, and I knew the drill. Any such act of violence had to be investigated, which would result in a ton of paperwork and many notifications.

I directed the switchboard operator to call for an ambulance. I notified the Borough Office. I wrote an entry in the log book. I scratched out an "Unusual Occurrence" statement and had the clerical staff type it up. I told the wagon operator to take off. It'd be a while.

He left laughing.

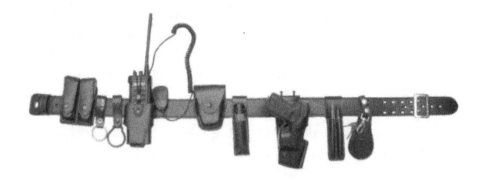

NOT ALL ADJUST TO THE 28 PRECINCT

There was an influx of new police officers assigned to the 28 Precinct. Some rode in a van with a veteran training officer. Others were put into radio cars with the two assigned officers. They would watch and learn. After a period, they were allowed to go on post alone.

Though they weren't really on their own. They were under the watchful eyes of the cops in the sector cars. I'm sure those experienced police officers remembered what it was like to walk a post. Especially on West 125.

You could ask me. Lieutenants still had the option of desk duty, riding as an onlooker in a sector car, or walking a post.

It was a nice day, so I figured I would take a walk on West 125 and check on the policemen assigned. Mind you, I was in full uniform.

As I crossed Eighth Avenue, I couldn't help but notice that people were giving me a look. Some not too friendly.

I managed to make it halfway up West 125 before I decided to return to the station house. I felt that I was antagonizing people, just walking alone in full uniform.

One police officer who was assigned to 125 Street on his

first day in the 28 Precinct confessed to me after he left the NYPD for the Nassau Police Department, he was going to turn in his shield. Born and raised in a different environment, he'd been surprised to find that police work ain't all peaches and cream.

There were at least seven female officers assigned to the precinct, and I'd have welcomed any one of them as a partner in a sector car.

But there was one, who, in my opinion, wasn't cut out to be a street cop and certainly not in the 28. She was a petite woman, very thin. In fact, she was so tiny, she couldn't wear all of the heavy equipment required by the department on her gun belt.

One day, she was assigned to West 125 and scheduled for a post change to court at nine. A sergeant found her, sitting in a sector car with the two officers assigned to the car. Their reasoning: *She's going to court in a little while, so why not have a seat until it's time to appear?*

In reality, they were doing what a lot of the veterans in the 28 did. They were keeping an eye out for the rookies until they got a little time under their belt.

When Sgt. Quinn on patrol approached the car, she got out. The guys from the sector car said, "She has a post change shortly to court."

He told them, "Get back on patrol." To her he said, "You, stay on post until your post change."

Now, I know Sergeant Quinn. I'm sure that what happened next was unintentional on his part.

He circled the block for no special reason, and there she was, sitting in a radio car. Not the same one. When she saw him, she jumped out of the sector car and stated running toward the station house!

She rushed past the desk and up to her locker room.

Shortly, Sgt. Quinn came in and explained to the desk officer about her running from him.

They both went up to the locker and knocked.

She screamed, "Get away from the door!"

They tried to reason with her but, since she was obviously quite upset and was in possession of a firearm, they retreated back to the desk.

They were discussing how to handle the situation, when she came down, wearing civilian clothes. They didn't stop her, just watched as she walked out the door and hailed a cab.

The desk officer notified all concerned. The story spread throughout the precinct.

The conclusion of this saga was that she was reevaluated, and they assigned her some clerical job, a few blocks from her home.

Oh, yeah—without her firearms.

COMPLAINT NUMBER THREE

The final shoe dropped. (How many shoes was that?) Anyway, I received the news, by department mail, that they were bringing me up on charges. I assumed the other lieutenants were also notified. I thought, *Hey, this is the third time I'll be going to the trial room. I'm batting .500.*

They found me guilty on the first. Not guilty on the second. Who was I kidding? It was a stacked deck. But truthfully, I wasn't worried. The department always threatened that, as punishment, they'd take away your detail. Which they did. Or take away some vacation days. Which they did. Or transfer you to a different precinct. Which they did. Or send you to Harlem—not just Harlem, but the 28 Precinct in Harlem. Which they did.

Now, when I talk to retired officers, the conversation always turns to your previous commands.

"Where'd you work?"

"The 14th."

"Lucky you. Then where?"

"The 23."

"Wow, Spanish Harlem! Then where?"

"Well, let's see. I was at OCCB for a few years, at a sewer called the 67 in Brooklyn, made lieutenant and went to Disney World, the 61, from there to Cecil Sledge's last command, the 69, and my last command before I retired, the 28."

"What!?"

Let me tell you all....

The 28 was the busiest in the city with probably more drug arrests than any other precinct. The personnel were loyal to each other and any slackers didn't last long.

The bosses were right out there with the men and didn't break your spirit with nonsense discipline. They have a chant in the backroom or in the locker room, "Who's better than the 28? No effing body!" And that's how I felt.

By the way, the loudest voice to praise the 28 was that of Officer Timmy Motto, president of the FOP 69. He was my conduit for passing the money from the card game to the deserving families. Now retired, he still attends functions where he champions the police, bucking heads with politicians and keeping the memory of Phil Cardillo alive. He's tireless!

The other lieutenants who were charged had accepted a negotiated plea. They would be docked two vacations days.

Then it was my turn.

I was informed of the negotiated plea. The charges were read, and I was asked, "How do you plead?

I didn't give an answer other than explaining the times

they worked, the unmarked car they used, and the civilian clothes they wore, and the difficulty in supervising them.

The Trial Commissioner was a little shocked and said, "Why don't you plead, 'Not Guilty?'"

I fell on my sword and admitted I was responsible for not verifying whether they signed out properly. I accepted the negotiated plea.

Sorry Barbara, I thought. *We won't be able to go to Paris this year.*

INTERNAL AFFAIRS

After I cleaned off the blood from the wounds I received in the trial room, I went back to work. I realized that I couldn't jeopardize over twenty years of police work and retirement benefits by being so cavalier in my approach to my responsibilities.

And it paid off.

I was doing a 4 to midnight on the desk when the switchboard operator told me, "Someone wants to talk to the desk officer."

I took the call, and it was a male voice. He told me he attended a party the previous night, and there was a police officer there, smoking dope.

"Do you know his name?" I asked.

"No."

"Can I have your name?"

"No."

"How did you know he was a police officer and that he was from this command?"

"I saw him in a police car."

"Could you describe him?"

"He was a male black, and that's all I'm going to say." He hung up.

Normally, this call would merit no action on anyone. Except a light bulb lit up over my head!

The call had come in with no background noise at all. Unusual? Not so unusual. While at OCCB, if we made a call that we wanted to record, we would use a sound proof office.

Was I being paranoid? We would see.

He had described a situation, where he obviously wanted to punish this "police officer." Yet he gave no useable information.

Ah-ha. A ruse by Internal Affairs to see if calls such as this would be reported or put in the round file (sometimes known in the navy as, "Deep six it," or better known as the most popular expression, "Shit can it").

I called Internal Affairs, made entries in the log, and then went back to reading the sports page.

Days later, a sergeant who had desk duty was brought up on charges for failing to report an allegation of a police officer smoking dope at a party. This sergeant was on the lieutenant's list. I never found out the results of the charge.

See, being paranoid paid off.

Allegations against police officers are usually reported and deemed substantiated or unsubstantiated and filed in the officers' records. These allegations are sometime frivolous and sometime serious. When reports of a certain type built up in an officer's record, an investigation would begin.

I'll give you an example of this....

A police officer came into the station house with a prisoner in handcuffs. He let the desk officer know what the charge would be and was told by the desk officer to search the prisoner in his presence.

Another policeman came up to the arresting officer, took him aside, and told him, "The guy you're locking up is a cop!"

Panic time!

He tried to leave the prisoner with another member of his team, so he could use the bathroom.

Internal Affairs stepped in, identified themselves to the desk officer.

It was explained that this officer, who made this arrest, was under suspicion of taking portions of the money that had been confiscated at the time of arrest. They had incriminating evidence because the arresting officer had a dye on his hands and on money found in his pockets.

Various charges would be filed against that officer.

This all came about because of the amount of complaints that were building up in his folder.

Another way that honesty was measured both while on patrol or in the station was a tired trick that Internal Affairs used to snare miscreants.

This happened to me while I was on desk duty in the 67 Precinct.

A well-dressed male brushed by security, placed a wallet on the switchboard and said, "I found this on the corner." Then he left.

I observed this, and I told the security officer, "Check this for ID and voucher it and any contents in it."

He looked in the wallet and said, "There's a 50-dollar bill in here."

I told him more sternly, "Voucher it *and* its contents."

A companion story to that one happened, while I was on patrol as a lieutenant in the 28.

We were on Central Park North (West 110 Street), and a lady approached our car and said, "I found this in the trash."

She dropped a women's pocketbook in my driver's lap and walked away.

"No, I wasn't going to jump out of the car and ask her any particulars. The address was right on West 110.

Now listen to this. We put ourselves out-of-service to return this pocketbook.

We knocked, and a lady came to the door.

I explained, "We have your purse. I assume it was grabbed and dumped after removing its contents."

She just stared at us and walked back in her apartment.

It turned out, the last time she'd seen that pocketbook, it was on a table in her hallway.

We walked in, and I checked the window off the fire escape.

Footprints on the window sill and on the toilet seat in the bathroom showed how someone had entered the apartment.

To get to the pocketbook, the thief had crawled past a bedroom where the elderly lady had been asleep. He had taken the purse and left the same way.

Thank God she hadn't discovered that bastard in her apartment!

TIME TO SAY GOODBYE

I've been there in the 28 for a few years, and although there'd been some bumps in the road now and then, I'd managed to stay out of trouble and harm's way until....

I was doing a 4 p.m. to midnight tour on the desk when in walks a loud, boisterous young man shouting obscenities to no one in particular.

The security officer stood by, awaiting instructions from me.

I let this young man have his say. Then I told him, "That's enough. Now calm down and tell me what's the problem."

He continued, and I made a move to my left, (the entrance was on my right) figuring he would take the hint to leave.

He didn't. He stood his ground.

I committed myself and told the officer on security, "I'll handle this."

I grabbed a handful of his jacket with the intention of

physically escorting him out.

Wow! Something gave out in my shoulder, and this young man must have seen the look of pain on my face, and he took off through the door.

I told the security guard, "Take me to the hospital."

I ended up with a sling. I fudged a story and got a sergeant to relieve me.

I called my wife and told her, "I'll be home early tonight."

A couple of cops drove me home, and Bobbie had coffee ready for us. I gave her a white lie story about how I'd hurt myself.

I stayed out for a few days and returned. Guess what? Half of the men knew how I'd hurt myself, and only Bobby DeLoose had the guts to tell me not to get involved, to let the security officer handle nonsense like that.

I realized he was saying, "Hey, you're too old for this stuff."

Ye Gads, I thought. *He's right.*

His advice was noted and filed away.

Then a terrible and unusual set of circumstances occurred, which caused the termination of four 28 Precinct police officers.

A group of men and woman came in to make a complaint about police officers who they said had entered a location that even they called, "a drug den."

I found out there were abandoned stores or apartments that were being used to inject drugs or sleep off the effects of narcotics.

The officers were alleged to have entered and confiscated drugs and taken money that belonged to the individuals there.

The desk officer took down the allegations and informed Internal Affairs. Supposedly, the switchboard operator had called one of the units and told them that a complaint had been made.

Internal Affairs brought charges. A department trial was

held. They played a tape of the switchboard operator and one of the units. They were suspended and, eventually, lost their jobs.

It was quite a shock to me because I was on desk duty, when they were suspended. There was paper work to be done. One of them had about 18 years on the job.

Most of the men in the command were aware of the results of the department trial. They were a bit down, but what was about to transpire would make them even more unhappy.

The department sent six newly promoted sergeants to our command for training. They would be with us for a few days, and a schedule would be set up beginning the next day. It would be the duty of the desk officer on this tour to assign them different tasks.

I introduced myself and gave each one a specific assignment. One would ride with the patrol sergeant. Another would work alongside the sergeant in charge of the SNEU. Two would ride in sector cars to observe and learn. One would work the desk alongside me. I told the sixth to sit in the muster room and observe the functions of the station house as a whole.

I was approached by Bobby DeLoose. He said, "Can I talk to you, Lieutenant?"

He told me that he'd written a better score than at least three of those new sergeants, and yet they'd been promoted ahead of him.

"Bobby, I know you've heard of affirmative action," I said. "Well, you're seeing it in action today."

I didn't have to explain that minorities in the department were given an edge in appointment. Where it used to be the higher the mark, the sooner you'd be called up a rank—not so anymore.

One of the new sergeants received a call and said, "It's the captain."

I went to the desk, took the phone and was told by the executive officer to stay by the desk. He said, "We don't want to give any of these new guys any bad ideas about how we run things around here."

I went back to talk to Bobby and Angelo, who was our wagon operator and a Vietnam veteran. Angelo told me, "I heard what you said to Bobby about this race thing. Watch yourself. You don't want to get a reputation. You know what I'm talking about?"

I walked past them, went to my locker and changed back into my street clothes. I was just about to leave, when the exec knocked and told me, "Jim, we have to walk on tiptoes around these guys."

It hit me like a brick that more than my reputation was at stake. So was my pension and my self-respect. For thirty years, I'd taken pride in the fact that I dealt with people according to their character, their words and actions toward others and me. I had never treated anyone differently because of their race, gender, religion, or anything else. And I wasn't going to start.

"Captain," I said, "don't worry about me. I'm going down to make an entry in the log that I have retired."

I went to the log and wrote: *2000 hours. Lieutenant James Cocalas retired, end of a thirty-year career.*

I got home in time to have tea and some toast with my wife. When I told her I'd retired, she said, "Thank you, Lord. Thank you."

Thank you, indeed!

RETIREMENT'S UPS AND DOWNS

The day after I put in my papers, I received a few calls from the precinct. Same question from all. "What happened?" Same answer. "I felt it was time to go."

Days later, they called again and told me, "The command wants to throw you a party."

I made it known to them strongly not to. "Just tell them I said, 'Who's better than the 28? No effing body!' Tell them I'm putting those things behind me. I'm going to sleep late, going to be home for Christmas, New Year's Day, Thanksgiving, July 4th, Easter Sunday, Howdy Doody's birthday. When it rains or snows, I'll be home having a cup of Joe. I'll be waiting for the mailman to deliver my pension check. My wife has put my uniform with the lieutenants' bars away, along with my bellbottom trousers from the time I spent in the navy."

That first week we traveled to Kannapolis, North Carolina, to visit her cousin, Ruth—the same Ruth who was with Bobbie back in 1953, when I first met the girl I would marry.

We made the rounds, visiting all her relatives. They are such a warm loving family. They had a family reunion to coincide with Barbara's birthday.

The local Baptist church offered their family room for the reunion. Everybody brought a dish to share with others. And they did something, which I'm ashamed I hadn't been doing in my household. They thanked the Lord for the food and asked Him to bless all present.

Everyone knew I was a police officer, and a New York one to boot! I really loved to watch their expressions when I related some of the horrible things I've seen or experienced. (I confess I exaggerate a little. But, of course, not in *this book*!)

Every time we visited, we attended the church that most of the family attends.

It took me awhile to realize why the churches down South are full on Sunday. They entertain first and preach later.

After church, Ruth, Bobbie, Louise, and her husband, Charlie, and I went out to eat. They'd all pile into my van and once they'd finally decided where we were going to eat, (It takes a while.) I'd take them there.

The food was really good and inexpensive.

Back at Ruth's house, she'd serve a cake that she'd baked before church.

I'd sit and shoot the bull with Charlie, and the ladies would sit in the kitchen and talk, laugh, and talk some more.

My wife loved it there, and the women would gang up on me to live there. My wife told them, "It's no use. He loves his Thursday card game more."

That is one of the reasons, but there are others. It is not only the card game.

In reality, because of that game, Barbara and I went to the Bahamas twice and Las Vegas twice, all within two years. And at no expense for all who came along.

I'll tell you how it worked.

We have a club in Brooklyn, and there are usually enough there to have two games going at once.

We take a cut of each pot and, at the end of six months, we give all an option to go on the trip or forfeit some of the money due them. Pasquale, the detective from the 67 Precinct, is a partner in a travel agency and handles all arrangements.

Bobbie and I didn't gamble but enjoyed the beach in the Bahamas, and the Las Vegas shows. I caught her one time at the slot machine. She couldn't deny it. She had smudges on her face from the coins.

This card game started in the 23 Precinct. You could say I encouraged guys to come to Brooklyn to play. With every precinct that I was assigned, I recruited. That includes OCCB, the 67, the 69, and the 28. The game started in 1969 and has continued till the present. Not the present as when I retired, but as the present in which I'm typing this!

I started taking money out of the pot until I reached $1000. It would take about six months to collect that much. Then I would reach out to police organizations, the Chaplain's Office, etc., to find a police family that was in need of some cash. Specifically, we looked for a family with a sick child.

I collected over $8,000, money that was then distributed. I made sure that the recipient emailed me, so I could show how the money had been distributed.

My wife always told me, "Don't take bows when doing good." But in this instance, I do, because it was like pulling teeth. Eventually, I stopped collecting. There was too much grumbling.

When down South visiting, Bobbie, Ruth and I would go antique shopping. We have never left a store without buying something.

"Jim, isn't this perfect for the living room?"
(No)
"Won't this look good in the hutch?"
(No)
Her "yes" and Ruth's "yes" always won out.
On the way back, we would stop at a Food Lion, (I think

that's the name) and buy about six jars of Duke's Mayonnaise and two dozen of bottles of Cheerwine. (I'm not sure of the name.) It's like a Dr. Pepper. All that would last until our next visit.

Over the years, we invited all her relatives to visit us. We'd buy tickets to a Broadway show, go to the Empire State Building, the Statue of Liberty, the Metropolitan Museum of Art, The Village, and after visiting Harlem, take a slow ride down Fifth Avenue, past St Patrick's Cathedral, Rockefeller Center, Times Square, through the Midtown Tunnel and home.

They slept good those nights!

A HOME LOST

I made it a point to visit Bobbie's relatives regularly, espe-cially Ruth. Ruth's daughter, Leila, is living in New Jersey with her husband, John. Leila makes sure to have her mom visit her, as she's concerned about her mother's health and wellbeing.

Leila would let Bobbie and me know when her mom was going to visit. There was no asking Bobbie twice. We'd pack an overnight bag and take off. It's about a three-hour ride there.

For several reasons, I never minded visiting John and Leila. Number 1: John always picked up the tab for breakfast. Number 2: He and I would go to Atlantic City while the ladies got caught up with their gossip and the dinner cooked.

John and I got about two hours action before Leila would call and say, "Dinner's ready!"

Number 3: Ruth always baked a coconut cake for dessert.

After dinner, while the ladies were cleaning up, John and I would go to his man cave and shoot pool, while watching any one of three massive TVs.

Now you know why I loved visiting Bobbie's relatives.

We'd sleep late, but instead of eating breakfast at the house, we'd have a cup of Joe and go to a combination luncheonette and bakery in Smithville.

Try as I might, I couldn't pay for breakfast. John insisted on picking up the check.

"Jim, don't let John pay again." That was Bobbie talking.

"Don't you dare, Jimmy!" That was Leila talking.

John was laughing. "I already paid for it."

It was the same scenario every time we visited. After breakfast, depending on the weather, we walked around Smithville. The ladies bought homemade jams or jellies. I'd buy Ruth something to take back to North Carolina.

One day, when we were back home, we received a frantic call from Ruth in North Carolina. They'd had a fire at Leila and John's home. Thank God they had gotten out all right.

It happened in the middle of the night. They were asleep when Leila heard the smoke alarm. She managed to get out through the front door, while John had to go out onto the porch and jump to a lower porch to escape.

The house was burnt to the ground.

Sadly, they lost one of their pet cats.

This is hard for me to write about. Yes, they were safe, but that house was designed by them and specially furnished by them. All of their family treasures and photos were gone forever. All John's business records, computer files, gone.

We drove there as soon as we heard. When Ruth said, "There was a fire," we couldn't imagine how bad it was.

They say, "Burnt to the ground," and it literally was!

When I walked with John into what had once been his man cave, I was standing on ashes.

They grow them strong down South. Leila and John assured Ruth they were fine. They got right to work on recovery.

The first few weeks, they stayed at a hotel. Then, John got busy and, with his business sense, jumped on his insurance company's back.

He managed, somehow, to get two full-length trailers on his property and from there, he coordinated the rebuilding of his home, bigger and better than the one that had burned down.

It took them many months of living in the trailer.

We visited and shared one of those trailers with Ruth. Leila brought her Mom up from North Carolina, so they could comfort each other. God bless them!

We would squeeze into John's car and go out to dinner. Try as I might I couldn't pick up the tab at the restaurant.

I can hear them now....

"Jim, don't let John pay again." That's Bobbie talking.

"Jim, don't you dare." That's Leila talking.

John's laughing. "I already paid the bill."

Man Accused of Killing Four in Dispute Over Rent

United Press International

TRAGEDY ON OUR BLOCK

I've been living in this house since 1972. I loved it from the first time the realtor told me it was for sale. I gave him a deposit on the spot. (I told you earlier that I never saw the inside and about how he kept shaking his head.)

I put my other house up for sale and, though we loved it and the neighbors, we felt it was time to go.

Once the wheels were in motion, I let my sister, Helen, know that we had bought a house closer to her and her husband, Mike. Helen had the same taste as Bobbie. I love her dearly, but I knew there was a tinge of jealousy on her part.

My sister, Tillie, thinks it stems from the fact that Helen was betrayed by her first husband and saw how Bobbie and I continued to grow in our love for each other.

She had a firsthand seat in watching the awkwardness of dropping Bobbie off at my parents. She saw me return to the ship, then as soon as possible, hurry back home. She saw how we persevered, got a basement apartment and stayed there while our two children were born. She was there when we bought our first house. She stayed with Bobbie when I rushed our beautiful ten-month-old baby, Stephen, to the hospital.

She stayed with Bobbie when we said goodbye to Stephen.

Then came the day when she was sitting in the back seat of the realtor's car with Bobbie, and we were all going in with him to see the inside for the first time.

It was better than I could have imagined.

The first thing I saw was the woodburning fireplace. There was a window seat. I pictured Bobbie and me sitting there, reading, with the sun shining over our shoulders.

There was a stairway with a beautiful stained-glass window halfway up and a turn that led to three bedrooms and a room, which could be a dressing room or a smaller bed room.

Needless to say, we loved it. And the first thing Helen said was, "Oh, Bobbie, I'm so jealous. It's beautiful."

And that's how I felt every night when I came home from whatever precinct I was working. Bobbie and I continued to improve it, she on the inside, me on the outside. We painted inside and the trim on the outside. We wallpapered together. (Guys, don't do it. Either pay to get it done or, if you're doing it together, keep your criticism to yourself.)

One warm day, I was mowing the lawn. I later had to hire people to do it, but I figured I'd do half one day and the other half the next day. I've done it many times before, but with the heat of the afternoon and the fact that I'd worked a late tour the night before, I felt beat.

I said to myself, *Stupid, take a break.*

I shut the mower off and laid down in the shade of one of the maples on my front lawn.

I must have dozed off, but then I heard a lady's voice say, "Mister, mister, are you all right?"

"Huh? No, no I'm fine, thanks. Just taking a nap."

"Oh, I'm so glad I thought you had a heart attack."

"Thanks again. She went on her way. Bobbie was at the front door. "Who was that?"

"Oh, some lady who thought I was dead."
"Huh?"

As tranquil as it was living here, evil intruded.

There was an old home that the owner had converted to a rooming house. Strictly illegal. Heck, I wasn't going to complain. I was too busy loving my home and trying to make it even better.

We cut down some pines that were too close to the house, after we discovered raccoons were eating on the porch and leaving poop for us to wash down. They had to go!

But back to that rooming house.

I knew that there were two middle-aged ladies living there (I've still got a cop's eye.) and an older guy who my son told me ran a pizza store on Broadway.

I knew there was one other. He was the proverbial disgruntled loser that life throws in your way from time to time. He had a beef with the landlady and, during the night, set fire to the porch area.

The way the building was constructed, it caused a chimney effect. (I spoke to the fire chief later.) The fire spread upward.

By that time the whole neighborhood was awake.

The two ladies were trapped on the second floor. Their next-door neighbor tried to use a ladder to help them, to no avail. He said they fell back into the rooms. The screams will haunt him for a long time.

There was a young couple, who had rented a shed-type structure close to the house. They were unharmed but they lost all that they owned.

We offered our home as a shelter for them and gave the fire chief access to our house and our phone.

A total of four people died as a result of the fire, and the son of a bitch who started it was sitting on the curb, watching it all happen.

A video was taken by investigators of everyone at the scene, and he was identified as the individual who was told by the landlady that he had to leave.

He was arrested and later convicted and sentenced to twenty-five years in prison.

Later, after all was said and done, we gave some clothes to that young couple, everybody left, and we cleaned up the river of mud from our front door to our kitchen.

But what I saw, once again, was the compassion and love displayed by my wife, Bobbie.

BOBBIE, DIAL 9-1-1

Ah. It was a warm summer night, and I was on my way home from a quiet 4 p.m. to midnight tour. No traffic on the Wantagh Parkway all the way to the Sunrise Highway. I kept going east for a couple of miles. I shut off the air conditioner in the car, rolled down the windows, and took a deep breath. I'm telling you the air is different out on Long Island. I've had that argument with most of the cops I know in the city. I call them, "cave dwellers."

(It's true. If you're reading this, and you're offended, I apologize.)

There's a price to pay for living in a one-family home out here. You know...property taxes, school taxes, heating costs.

But when I would pull into my driveway, shut the engine off and sit back with the windows open, and smell fresh cut grass, or catch a whiff of wisteria—and best of all, listen to the quiet—it is well worth it!

But not that night.

My wife greeted me at our back door, and we sat for a while, talking about nothing. "Want some iced tea?" she asked.

After drinking our tea, we went inside to watch the end of a movie.

She sat up suddenly. "Did you hear that?" she said. "Sounds like somebody's out by the garage."

I went into the darkened downstairs bathroom. Sure enough, there were two figures by my son's F85 Cutlass (I gave it to him, and he insisting on modifying it.) It was sitting on blocks.

I told Bobbie to dial 9-1-1.

I grabbed an ornamental night stick and my off-duty gun and went out to the backyard.

Sure enough, there were two guys, standing to one side of the car.

When I confronted them, they ran.

They already had one of the tires off, but when they rolled it across the wet grass, it left a track right to a station wagon just around the corner.

There was the tire in the back of the vehicle. I stayed there by the car, and yelled as loud as I could, "Okay, stupid! I called the police."

Out from behind our neighbor's house came a stocky and cocky teenager with no shirt and no shoes.

He yelled, "Get away from my car!"

I told him, "Listen I'm a police officer, and I've already called the police. So, do yourself a favor and stay where you are."

I had the nightstick along my right side. The gun was in my back pocket.

He came toward me.

I swung the night stick across his knees, and he went down howling.

I stepped on his chest and hit him a love tap on his head.

My neighbor, a beloved pediatrician, came out of his home smoking a pipe.

I said, "Doc, go inside."

Then the cavalry came charging across my lawn, toward me and the tough guy lying in the street. They took pictures of the tire in his car and returned it to me. They shoved him into one of the police cars. Would you believe this jerk gave them a hard time? But not for long.

They hustled him to the police station. I went and gave them my story of what happened.

By the way, the other culprit was his 14-year-old brother.

His mother showed up at the station house and mumbled to me, "You'd probably lock up your mother."

The first time I'd heard that was when I'd found a little girl about three years old, walking the streets at 3 a.m. in the morning in alphabet city in New York (Avenue A, Avenue B, and so on).

When I got out of the car to talk to her, she ran into a building. I followed her to an open door, which was, no doubt, her apartment.

I'll describe the place the way I did in court in the presence of her mother, who was later arrested after she came to the station house to report her child missing.

"Your Honor, there was feces on the floor, roaches on the table, spoiled food in the refrigerator, an open container of spoiled milk. The door was open. No adults were present."

As I left the witness box and walked past the woman, she mumbled, "You'd probably lock up your mother."

Trash or Garbage?

YEAH, YOU'RE WELCOME

Still talking about my moving to this quiet, peaceful neighborhood....

Things went along smoothly, until the town decided that all the homes must hook up to the new sewer system they were putting in.

We had been here for a while, and we had cesspools which did overflow. So, I was glad it was being done, except that when they dug a trench along the avenue to lay the pipe, they hit water.

They had to put in pumps, large ones, run by generators, to pump the water out, and they were on 24 hours a day.

One of them was directly across from our bedroom.

They encased them in plywood to cut down on the noise. It didn't help. After a while, you seemed to get immune to the drone of the generators.

My neighbor across the street must have been going nuts from the noise. When we first moved in, the lady of the house (not my house, but my neighbors' house) approached me as I was putting out the trash. I had always called it, "garbage," but since moving here, I'd learned to call it, "trash."

She said, "Why don't you move your trash parallel to ours so the sanitation truck will only have to stop once to pick up both?"

"Huh?"

I was going to say something else but thought I'd better not.

I just gave a slight wave and went inside, thinking to myself, *From now I'm going to call it garbage*!

There would be no relief for her regarding the noise.

My son was working on our car and decided to change the spark plugs, whether they needed to be changed or not.

(In fact, as I'm writing this, I just asked him if he remembers our neighbor coming in the driveway while he was doing it. He told me he changed the wires, not the plugs, causing her television to buzz.)

Poor women. What she must have been thinking about this new family that dared to move into her neighborhood?

Sort of reminds me of when my family moved from the tenements in Williamsburg to the tree-lined block in Flatbush in 1941. My dad would sit in our backyard after work and have his coffee and smoke his Camel cigarettes. Our next-door neighbor would walk from her yard on our left to visit our neighbor on our right. There were no fences between our homes. She always had a cocktail glass in her hand. She would walk right in front of my dad, completely ignoring him.

My father, Old World gentleman that he was, never complained...until my mom was sitting with him one day, and our neighbor walked past them and completely ignored my mother. My father confronted her and, in a polite but firm way, told her not to come into our yard again.

Bravo, Dad.

Well, I'm an old softy. So, I told my son to change the wires to ones that wouldn't interfere with our neighbors' television. (And also ours.)

This particular couple lived in a world much different from my wife's and mine. They ignored us, and we did likewise.

However, fate and the fact that I was a police officer brought us together.

It seemed they were always visiting, or eating out, or going on vacation, and leaving their home unguarded, unprotected, empty.

One evening, I was out walking my miniature schnauzer, Tinker, and I saw a teenager sitting on a brick wall on the corner of my neighbor's property.

It didn't smell right to me.

I put Tinker back in the house and went to a mud room by my front door. I heard this teenager talking to someone I couldn't see, but I heard him say, "Let me in."

He went around to the back of the house.

I couldn't see him from where I was, but I had seen and heard enough!

I dialed 9-1-1 and gave the info that there was a burglary going down at my neighbors' home. I told them that I was a New York City police officer and would meet whoever responded at the intersection.

I told Bobbie, "I think someone's breaking into our friendly neighbor's home."

"Stay here!" she said. "Jim, please be careful!"

Within minutes, an unmarked police vehicle responded with only one guy in it!

I told him, "I'll watch the back, and you wait until more help arrives."

In another couple of minutes, marked police cars appeared.

I heard someone yell, "Don't move!"

Now...I was not where I should have been. I should have been home, sitting, watching TV with my wife, and not in civilian clothes in a darkened part of a yard with cops looking for the second burglar.

Whoosh!

Here came a figure, and there went a figure, running right past me.

He ran through that pediatrician's yard. (I told you about him earlier.) There was no way I was going to try and stop him.

I can't swear to it, but I think I knew who it was.

The uniformed officers arrested the one in the house, and I heard later that he was the rogue son of a Nassau County police officer.

They never arrested anyone else.

In a few days, our neighbors returned. And in a night or two, I heard my wife say to someone at the door, "Come in. Jim, our neighbor's here."

He walked in while I was watching TV, thanked me, gave me a bottle of scotch, and left.

I don't think we've said more than ten words to them since.

And besides, I don't like scotch.

MY FRIEND, LEO

Hello. Is this Moishe's Deli? How's the pastrami? No good? How come? Listen, I need your ladder. Yeah, I know it's in the garage. I'll get it. No, don't worry about your car. Just open the garage door. I'll bring it back later. The pine needles are clogging up my gutters."

I took my van around the corner to my friend's house. The garage door was open. and the ladder was hanging behind his van.

I squeezed between his van and the wall, slowly picked up the ladder, and maneuvered it over his hood.

I put it in my van and was just about to pull out, when my buddy opened the screen door and yelled, "That's three to your one."

I shouted back, "I'll see you later."

When I got home Bobbie asked me, "How's he doing?"

"All right," I told her. "He says he's ahead three to one."

She laughed.

He and I have a list of the amount of favors we do for each other. I use his tools and his ladder. Sometimes, I need to cut some wood with his band saw or have him do some electric voodoo on equipment that quit on me.

He calls me to help him bring things into his house that are too big or too heavy to carry while pushing his wheel chair. (Oh, didn't I tell you he's been in that wheel chair, unable to walk since 1968. In Vietnam a sniper's bullet severed his spine.)

One day, Bobbie and I were planting wild flowers in a rock garden behind our garage. They came up for a couple of years, but in the end, the weeds won out.

That morning, Bobbie called me over to a fence that intersects four properties. We peeked over, and there was this guy in a wheelchair, bent over and with only a hand spade, he was putting in bushes. Big bushes.

Bobbie whispered, "Why don't you ask him if we can help?"

We didn't even know the names of any families adjourning our property. We weren't antisocial, just busy fixing up the house, plus my screwball hours with the police department.

"Hi, ya doing fellow? Need a hand?" I asked.

He looked up, and I said, "This is my wife, Bobbie. I'm Jim. We live next door to you.

"Hi, Bobbie, Jim," he said. "I'm Leo. As a matter of fact, I have another plant in the back of my van."

"I'll get it." I walked past Bobbie on the way to his van and whispered to her, "Thanks a lot."

Thus, began a friendship that is still going on. However, I'm now up one to his nothing. I'm sure that will change soon.

As we got to know Leo better, we were always amazed at how he's overcome so much and how he's so independent.

When he had to be out, he went out. Nothing stopped him. He drove a specially modified van, and he and I would go to Atlantic City monthly.

I gave him directions to my Thursday night card game in Brooklyn, and for months, he played there.

The guys went overboard on meeting him. Most of us had been in the service, and I'm sure we all thought this guy was someone special.

Early on, he became a computer fanatic, and any time I needed help I would reach out to him. (That's one for him.) I helped to assemble his computer furniture. (That's one for me.)

I always made it a point to visit him or call him. "Hallo, is a'this Gino? I want a peppers and eggs hero. What? This is no Gino? Then why you answer the phone, you dope?"

I talked him into coming to visit our Baptist church. He's a devout Catholic. (No, I couldn't convert him.) And he got to know the pastor and his family.

On the occasion of putting up our church's first flag pole, thanks to me, (I can hear my wife saying, "Stop taking bows.") we invited him to raise our flag.

We have a few men in the church who go for breakfast on Tuesday at a diner. He's become one of those men. However, he got upset when I made remarks that he thought were offensive about the Pope. When he didn't attend one Tuesday, I asked him why. He mentioned my comments, and I surely didn't want to lose his friendship, so I apologized.

Shortly after that, we went to Atlantic City and in a card game called "Caribbean Stud" I was dealt a straight flush. (If you don't know what the odds are of being dealt that hand, look it up.) I won fifteen thousand dollars! Could it have been my apology? Naw.

Living alone in his condition may not seem like a big deal. But in truth, it's dangerous. Leo has a moving stairway to his basement. One day, while he was going down, the darn thing stopped. He was stuck!

He and I had discussed this type of an emergency before, and I'd suggested he take a phone with him.

He called. "Jim, I'm stuck."

When I got there he told me, "There's an emergency release at the base of the lift."

I told him I'd have to climb over him.

As I did, my manhood was sitting on his head. "Don't move!" I said.

I managed to make it over him and got him down.

Soon, we had the lift going again.

We both laughed and made some funny remarks that I probably shouldn't repeat here.

The next time he called, it was more serious. He was going downstairs on the lift, carrying too much. And when it came to a stop, he continued to roll forward. He fell and broke his leg.

He called, and I came. He ended up in a hospital.

That wasn't the last time he had to be hospitalized.

As I'm typing this, he is currently in the Bronx Veterans Hospital. I keep our congregation informed and always say a prayer for him.

Lord, he's had his share of grief.

FORGIVENESS

ೲೞ

How can I ask forgiveness of someone who is not with me anymore?

Nor did I think I had to.

It took me a long time to realize how selfish I was during my marriage to that 18-year-old.

As I told you in the beginning of this book, I met Barbara Smith when she was 17. Four months later, just after her mom died, we were married in a brief ceremony with only the deacon and pastor present.

A grueling twelve-hour bus ride and a few days in my parents' house was our "honeymoon," not to mention my mother demanding to see our wedding license.

I've asked her so many times to forgive me for that, but she's not here.

I had to get back to the ship, and I left her there while the rest of the family came to meet her. I've asked her so many times to forgive me for that, but she's not here.

Only recently, did I realize what a culture shock that was for her. Barbara came from a family that said grace before each meal. Her family would attend church together every Sunday. She attended Bible school. While in high school, she was the leader of the students' Bible study.

I discovered later that, when she came to meet me in Portsmouth, she brought her Bible that her mom bought for her. I looked at it recently and there was a notation that, on April 1952, she declared that Jesus Christ was her Savior.

My God, we didn't even have a Bible in our home.

I remember her asking me to pray with her when we were at our basement apartment. I prayed with her, but my heart wasn't in it.

I continued to live my life, doing what I thought I had to do—put food on the table, protect my family. And I continued to do that, especially after our Florence, our first, was born.

When James Anthony was born, I continued to do what I thought a man must do.

In a year or two, my second son Phillip was born. I went to the hospital to see Bobbie. She was resting. I went to where the newborn babies were, and Phillip wasn't there. They had him in an incubator.

Even then, I wasn't worried. I went back to my wife's room. Bobbie wasn't awake yet. I was called out to an office and was told Phillip didn't make it.

I loved her more than ever that day. But what happened that day pushed me further from God.

We bought a home in Laurelton. Bobbie enrolled the children in Christ Lutheran, an elementary school run by a man named Pastor Dinkel.

Bobbie took a job at E. J. Korvettes. We were a happy family. We all worked to make it the prettiest on the block.

Bobbie was expecting and, shortly, we welcomed our new son, Stephen. He was born the same day as his mommy, September 18!

The kids loved him.

Those were the happiest days for me. Bobbie was that same innocent, lovable person I married. I remember when I would come home from a 4 p.m. to midnight tour, and Stephen was asleep in his crib, I would go up to our room to look at him and take his hands and kiss them.

I was working an 8 a.m. to 4 p.m. tour. When I got home, Bobbie was lying on the couch asleep, and Stephen was in a bassinet alongside her.

The baby wasn't breathing right. I got my neighbor next door and rushed him to the hospital.

Bobbie, my sister, Helen, and Mike showed up just as the doctors came out and said, "Stephen didn't make it."

He was 10 months old.

Oh my God, why? I thought. *Please wake me up from a nightmare.*

A light went out in Bobbie's eyes after that.

We had a wake. All I can remember is my father standing by the little, white, closed casket and staring at it.

Somehow, we continued on. We bought a home on the island. I put all that grief behind me. Bobbie must have bottled it up.

We didn't stop living. We traveled to California, Niagara Falls, visited Bobbie's relatives down South, went to weddings, the beach, and on occasion into the city to see a play when her relatives visited.

I hadn't felt any tension between us, until one night. She fell asleep on the couch. I sat in my chair, watching her.

I had unloaded my gun the night before, as I always did when teenagers visited my kids.

When I was getting ready to leave, I was loading the gun and a round fell to the floor. I saw her look at it and at me, and she said, "Is that for me?"

I'd never seen her like that.

I reached out to my health group for advice, and they asked if I thought she might hurt herself. I said, "I don't know."

They suggested that I get in touch with Mercy Hospital.

I made arrangements to take her there. I did, with no resistance from Bobbie.

I asked the Lord again, *Why is this happening to her? Why Lord?*

She was there for a couple of weeks.

I sat in on a conference with therapists and with Bobbie. They explained that I was concerned with everything but her! I resisted but, after a few more meetings, I realized they were so right. Yeah, I put food on the table, protected them, but when Bobbie would offer a suggestion, she said I would just fluff it off.

I've asked her to forgive me so many times for that, but she's not here.

The years passed. We had our grandchildren visit on Sundays with Bobbie cooking sauce, meatballs and ziti or spaghetti. Before each meal we would hold hands and say, "God is great, God is good. Let us thank him for our food. Amen."

The grandkids were being taught. Something I should have done with my kids.

Bobbie found a Baptist church. (I passed that church every

day or night coming home from work.) She also attended a Bible study with the pastor's wife and other ladies from church. I would sometimes pick her up, waiting outside in my car.

A couple of the men came out and invited me in. One of them was a retired detective. His son-in-law is a police officer in the First Precinct and knew a friend of mine who works there with him.

I resisted until I read some notes from her Bible study. In the margin she had written: *I wish Jim would come to church.*

I could never refuse her again.

I sat and observed the people, especially the pastor and his family. It took me months before I went with my Bobbie to that church, but the simplicity of the sermon made a big impression on me—plus Bobbie squeezing my hand.

Over time, we really got involved with the church. Bobbie became part of the Sunshine Committee. We decorated, bought flowers and planted more flowers outside. I was voted in as a trustee. But that was many years ago.

Since then, Bobbie's health slowly declined, so we could not continue. I still ask for her forgiveness, but she's not here anymore.

After 63 years of marriage, my Bobbie passed away on November 11, 2017.

Dear Jim

We've passed so many forges
over 38 years. We were just kids
when we met, really. I remember
first seeing you and being so much
in love with you.

Boy, have we come a long
way! It hasn't all been good but
the bad times have only made us
stronger & better.

We've built a family, shared a
mother, and laughed with joy and
pride at our grandchildren. Shared
our childrens happiness & pain and
spent a few sleepless nights

Thank you for letting me be generous
with them all & not complaining
about my obvious faults. Thank you
for being there when I needed you
most. Too many good times cloud
my mind to write them all down.
But there has never been a time
in my heart that I haven't loved
you just like that silly school girl
you married so many years ago.

Thank You for sharing my life,
Happy Anniversary — Bobbie

SEASONS

How wonderful the summer sun is, warming my bones, dimming the memory of the bitter cold, which penetrated my skin and chilled my blood last winter.

Yet, while walking with the snow crunching beneath my feet and my breathe steaming from my mouth, how refreshing the cold air is, as I suck it deep into my lungs, allowing me to push out of my mind's corner those hot, humid nights that stole my sleep.

What could be more promising than spring, budding trees, and the green softening of the earth, bringing dreams of upcoming outings?

And yet, when the first cool day of fall comes, I regret not the passing of the last months, but look ahead, inviting the turning of the leaves, the smell of wood burning. And while rummaging around, looking for a light jacket to wear, seeing Christmas decorations packed in the corner, I let my mind drift a bit to the upcoming holiday and feel that everything is in its proper place, as He wants it.

Jim Cocalas

F

ON THE JOB

Supervising the Removal of a Body

Disorderly in a Bank

Drunk Driver, Hit and Run on Eighth Avenue

Pier Strike Agitator

Helicopter Rescue Heroes

Robbery Attempt Foiled, Two Shot (by Guy with Hanky)

ABOUT THE AUTHOR

Thrice decorated, twice commended by the FBI, Jim Cocalas served and protected the citizens of New York City for thirty years as a patrolman, sergeant and lieutenant. Some fortunate people, their children, and grandchildren walk those city streets today because he put his own life in jeopardy to save theirs.

He patrolled the Big Apple's poorest and most dangerous neighborhoods with compassion, borne of deep understanding, having been raised in similar circumstances.

After spending his childhood in a tough area of Brooklyn, during the Depression, cursed with poverty, but blessed with the love of family, Jim believes he "was growed up lucky." Although, reading his memoirs, one might consider him lucky to have "growed up" at all.

During the Korean War, Jim joined the U.S. Navy and served his country aboard the world's largest ship of its day, the USS Midway. He travelled the world from the Arctic Circle to the Mediterranean, Guantanamo Bay to Gibraltar, Haiti to Nova Scotia, and many ports beyond.

Now, with his service to country and the people of New York finished, his children raised, and his beloved wife at rest, Jim is pouring his considerable energies into yet another career. As an author, he shares his countless stories, heartbreaking and joyful, in an effort to inform his readers about what it means to serve as a police officer.

CPSIA information can be obtained
at www.ICGtesting.com
Printed in the USA
BVHW04s0105100718
521263BV00005B/24/P